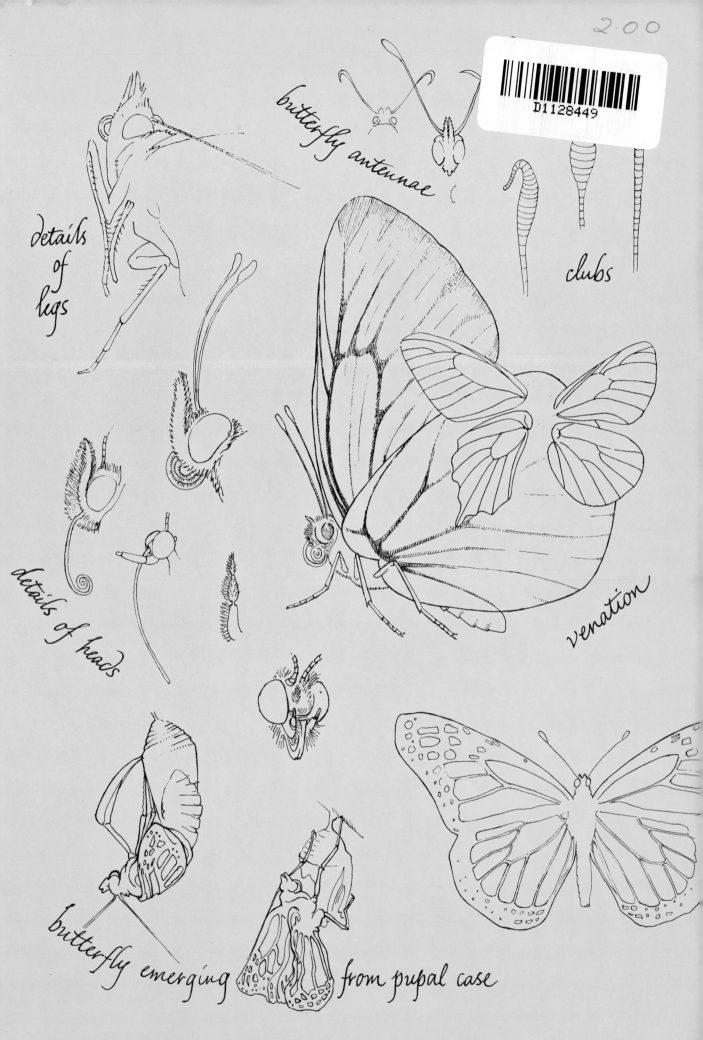

details of legs

butterfly antennae

clubs

details of heads

venation

butterfly emerging from pupal case

Butterflies

A GOLDEN BOOK OF

187 Familiar North American Butterflies

Butterflies

By J. F. GATES CLARKE, Ph.D.

Head Curator, Department of Entomology
Smithsonian Institution

Illustrated by
ANDRÉ DURENCEAU

Under the editorship of
HERBERT S. ZIM, Ph.D.

GOLDEN PRESS NEW YORK

Contents

Foreword

This introductory book on butterflies, best known and most attractive of insects, has been a pleasant task to write. It is an invitation to young and old to learn about the more common North American butterflies. Besides reading, try to observe the butterflies directly and study the species that you are sure to find in your own neighborhood.

Nearly all the colored illustrations in the book are by Andre Durenceau, adapted from the plates made for Butterflies and Moths, a Golden Nature Guide. The end sheets are by Anne Scott. Robert Mitchell spent many hours obtaining material on caterpillars for the artist. William D. Field selected and prepared the museum specimens. Our special thanks are due to the Smithsonian Institution, Washington, D.C. for lending the specimens to the artist. Thanks also go to Mary Irving, who helped with the editorial work.

J.F.G.C.

Introduction

Butterflies and moths belong to a large group or order of insects known as Lepidoptera, which means scale-wing. The name comes from two Greek words, *lepis*, meaning scale, and *pteron*, meaning wing. Lepidoptera is only one of 24 orders of insects but it is the only group that has scaled wings. Lepidoptera includes two large groups. Both are well known—the moths and the butterflies. These in turn are classified into many smaller groups known as families. For instance, the swallowtail butterflies belong to the family Papilionidae, which contains approximately 500 kinds, or species. Each family of butterflies is further divided into *genera*, such as *Polygonia*, the angle wings. Each *genus* contains one or more closely related species. Sometimes butterflies are further divided into races, or varieties. Thus, every butterfly, indeed every living thing, has at least two names—the *genus* name and the *species* name. The butterfly which is known as the Mourning Cloak is known scientifically as *Nymphalis antiopa*. This is the kind of scientific name you will find for each butterfly illustrated in this book.

Most people can tell butterflies and moths apart. You see butterflies mainly in the daytime and moths at night. But this day and night flying habit does not hold for all butterflies and moths. So look also at the antennae which stick out from the butterfly's head. If they are clubbed, you can be quite sure you see a butterfly. Moths generally have feathered or thread-like antennae.

To distinguish one species of butterfly from another is a different story. There is no single way to do this. The size, the color, the markings are all important. Scientists pay attention to the details of the wings, legs, antennae and mouthparts. Many of the common butterflies are so clearly marked you can identify them

RUDDY COPPER
Lycaena rubidus

PURPLISH COPPER
Lycaena helloides

AMERICAN COPPER
Lycaena phlaeas americana

Here are three closely related butterflies. Their scientific names show they belong to the same genus, though each is a different species.

MARINE BLUE
Leptotes marinus

SQUARE-SPOTTED BLUE
Philotes battoides

HARVESTER
Feniseca tarquinius

Here are three less closely related butterflies. All six above belong to the same family, Lycaenidae, but each of the lower three belongs in a different genus.

11

MOTHS are, for the most part, night flying Lepidoptera with large and plump bodies. They rest with their wings extended flat or folded roof-like over their backs. In North America there are at least ten times as many kinds of moths as butterflies.

IO MOTH

after you have seen their pictures. In some kinds the males differ from the females, and occasionally those which hatch early in the season look a bit different from those which hatch out later. With experience you can usually identify your species.

Naming the butterfly is just one step. If you have a chance to watch it grow, you will learn much more about it and will find out what an unusual insect it is. Butterflies go through four stages of development, each distinctly different. The adult female butterflies lay eggs from which the caterpillars, or larvae, hatch. The body of the caterpillar, including the head, normally has thirteen segments. The next three segments, or rings, after the head each bear a pair of legs. In addition, each caterpillar has four pairs of *prolegs* on segments six to nine, and another pair on the last segment. The prolegs are fleshy and each ends in a series of little hooks with which the caterpillar clings to plants as it feeds. Many of the details of the structures of butterflies in all the stages of development are sketched on the end sheets at the front and back of this book.

BUTTERFLIES, with small, slim bodies, fly by day. When they rest they usually hold their wings together, high over their backs. Larvae of both butterflies and moths feed mainly on plants but only a relatively few species (mainly moths) do serious damage to crops.

MOUNTAIN FRITILLARY BUTTERFLY

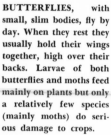

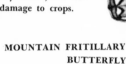

antennae of moth   scales of moth

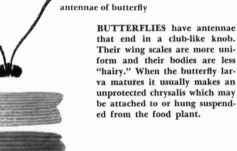

antennae of butterfly

BUTTERFLIES have antennae that end in a club-like knob. Their wing scales are more uniform and their bodies are less "hairy." When the butterfly larva matures it usually makes an unprotected chrysalis which may be attached to or hung suspended from the food plant.

MOTHS often have feathery antennae. The scales on the wings and body are variable, often thin and "hairy." When the larvae of moths are mature they often spin a silken cocoon in which they pupate, or the larvae may form their pupae in underground cells or in debris.

scales of butterfly

MOURNING CLOAK
chrysalis

QUESTION MARK
chrysalis

CECROPIA MOTH cocoon

AILANTHUS SILK MOTH cocoon

MONARCH BUTTERFLY
chrysalis

The skin of the caterpillar may be smooth or ornamented with spines, horns or tubercles. As it grows, the caterpillar sheds its skin from time to time and is said to *molt*. From the hatching of the egg to the time the pupa, or chrysalis, is formed the larva usually molts four times. Most caterpillars feed on some plant or group of plants on which the butterfly lays its eggs. One kind of caterpillar feeds on small insects.

When the larva has fed and grown for a certain period of time, it enters a resting period to form the pupa, or chrysalis, the third stage in a butterfly's life. Usually the pupa, or chrysalis, is suspended by a button of silk from some overhanging object, such as a branch or twig. The forms of the chrysalis vary greatly, although each family of butterflies has a rather distinctive kind. Most pupae are pale or dull colored but some are decorated with brilliant metallic spots.

The changes that take place in the pupa may be accomplished in only a few weeks. Many butterflies, however, spend the winter in the pupal stage and so hibernate for six months or more. Whatever the time taken, the internal changes are tremendous. A complete reorganization changes the wormlike, wingless caterpillar into a four-winged adult. Few other changes in nature are as complicated and as little understood as this one.

The chrysalis splits down the back and the adult butterfly emerges. Wings are crumpled and folded, but the adult pumps blood through channels in the wings, stretching and extending them. When the wings are expanded, the channels harden to form veins. Soon the adult can fly and is off in search of a mate.

A few adult butterflies do not feed at all, dying soon after they mate and lay their eggs. Others live as adults for about a year, feeding on the nectar of flowers and, in some cases, migrating to spend the winter in warmer climates.

Very few butterflies are of direct importance to people. Some caterpillars feed on crops, like

adult

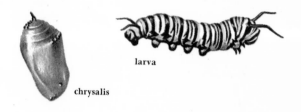

chrysalis

larva

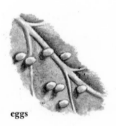

eggs

THE MONARCH BUTTER-FLY, like all others, goes through a life cycle that includes four distinct stages. The small ribbed, cone-like eggs are laid on milkweed. The small larva that emerges from each egg feeds voraciously on the milkweed leaves, molting as it grows. When it is mature, it attaches itself to the plant and forms a shining green chrysalis. In the chrysalis a tremendous change takes place to form the winged adult butterfly that finally emerges.

the cabbage white which attacks cabbage, and the alfalfa butterfly which attacks alfalfa. Most butterflies are helpful as well as beautiful, aiding in the pollination of flowers.

The list of books on page 66 are mainly simple introductions to this group of well-known insects and elementary guides to their field identification. In addition, the reader will find scores of books on insects, including entomology texts with sections on Lepidoptera. Books in this list marked (Y) are particularly recommended for younger readers.

Swallowtails

The swallowtails and parnassians make up a big family found over a large part of the world. This group of more than 530 colorful species includes the largest and most spectacular butterflies known. Most are tropical, but even in temperate regions swallowtails are striking and beautiful.

Of the two groups, the swallowtails are by far the largest—about 500 different kinds. Only about 20 species live in North America. Not all swallowtails have "tails" at the ends of their hind wings. The Pipevine and Polydamas Swallowtails are closely related. The Pipevine has a tail; the Polydamas has none. The Pipe-

vine caterpillar looks dangerous but it is not; it only appears that way because of the thin, fleshy spikes that cover its body. When the caterpillar has finished feeding, it changes into a pupa (from the Latin word for puppet or doll), or chrysalis (from the Greek word meaning gold, because of the golden color of some butterfly pupae). The chrysalis of this and other swallowtail butterflies is attached to the plant on which it feeds, or to some other object, by a threadlike strand of silk which passes around the pupa. The rough-looking chrysalis of the Pipevine Swallowtail has bumps on its back.

PIPEVINE SWALLOWTAIL
Battus philenor
3.0-4.5"

male

PIPEVINE
SWALLOWTAIL
larva

PIPEVINE
SWALLOWTAIL
pupa

male

POLYDAMAS SWALLOWTAIL
Battus polydamas
3.0-4.0"

14

Wherever its food plant, the pipevine, grows in the United States the Pipevine Swallowtail is found. It is said to be distasteful to birds—at least birds do not eat it. Certain other butterflies protect themselves by imitating or mimicking the form and color of the Pipevine Swallowtail.

The Polydamas Swallowtail lives in southern United States. Its caterpillar feeds on plants related to pipevine.

When new adults of the Palamedes Swallowtail emerge in May, the dark areas of their wings are sooty-black with creamy-yellow markings. These colors soon fade so that by mid-June the butterflies look dull and worn. However, a new brood soon emerges, and by July brilliantly colored adults are again on the wing. Palamedes Swallowtails favor swampy land or moist woods where the caterpillar feeds on magnolia and sassafras.

The Giant Swallowtail is the largest butterfly in the United States. It has a wide range because the larva, or caterpillar, feeds on a variety of plants, among them prickly ash, hop tree, and citrus. In Florida the caterpillar is called the "orange puppy" because it feeds on orange leaves. The caterpillar is smooth, and is not covered with spikes like the larva of the Pipevine Swallowtail. The pupa has no large humps on it.

When the wings of certain butterflies are placed in contact with a photographic plate or cut film, they produce an exposure which results in a perfect image of the butterfly wing. The Giant Swallowtail is one of about 40 butterflies—at least 8 of them swallowtails—that are known to produce such an effect. Catch one and you can demonstrate this for yourself, if you have the time and patience. The photographic plate or film must be kept in the dark and the butterfly wing applied with even pressure to the shiny, coated side of the plate. Sometimes exposures can be made in 12 to 24 hours, but it is best to leave the wing in place for a week to bring out the pattern. The more recent the specimen, the brighter the image.

PALAMEDES SWALLOWTAIL
Papilio palamedes
4.5-5.5"

GIANT SWALLOWTAIL
Papilio cresphontes
4.0-5.5"

GIANT SWALLOWTAIL larva

ALASKAN SWALLOWTAIL
Papilio machaon aliaska
2.8-3.0"

male

BLACK SWALLOWTAIL
Papilio polyxenes
2.8-3.5"

male

female

The Alaskan Swallowtail is a subspecies of a butterfly found in northern Asia and Europe. The subspecies is found in Alaska and Canada. Many butterflies, including the Alaskan Swallowtail, send out a scent or odor produced by special scent scales. The odor is sweet-smelling, not unlike the scent of carrot flowers.

The caterpillar of the Alaskan Swallowtail has alternating rings of black and green that encircle the body. The black rings have a pair of orange-yellow spots on the back. The caterpillar eats carrot and sagebrush.

Like other swallowtails, the full-grown caterpillar spins a pad of silk on the stem it has selected as a place for its chrysalis. It crawls up over it and fastens its claspers to the pad, head uppermost. The larva then bends its head and the first few segments of its body sideways, attaching a strand of silk to one side of the stem. Then it twists around, passing the silk thread over its back, and fastens the strand to the other side of the stem. After this has been repeated several times, a slender silken loop is formed strong enough to support the chrysalis.

The caterpillar then goes into a short resting period. Its skin, which has become too tight for the growing caterpillar, splits down the back. After much wriggling, the skin slips down toward the tail and the chrysalis emerges.

The Black Swallowtail, a close relative of the Alaskan Swallowtail, is the only one of this group found east of the Continental Divide. It produces two broods. Adults may be seen from late April until October, occasionally until mid-November. All the other members of the group live in the western part of the continent.

Like some of the other swallowtails, the Black Swallowtail appears in several color forms. In one form, the middle row of yellow spots on the fore and hind wings is narrow; in another form it is wide. Sometimes the black center of the orange spot of the hind wing is missing. The female differs from the male by having tiny yellow spots as the inner row.

The Black Swallowtail does not like the woods. It is always found in open country where its rapid, darting flight sets it off from other similar swallowtails. Flowers are a great attraction to it. Although these swallowtails pause frequently to feed, their wings keep in nervous motion all the time.

Sometimes the Black Swallowtail is called the Parsnip Swallowtail because the caterpillar feeds on that plant. Often the butterflies are found in gardens where carrots, celery and parsley are grown. The caterpillars feed on all wild and cultivated plants of the carrot family.

Baird's Swallowtail, a western species, is quite similar to the Black Swallowtail of the eastern United States. The caterpillar feeds on

16

ANISE SWALLOWTAIL
Papilio zelicaon
2.5-3.5″

Tail lengths compared

INDRA SWALLOWTAIL
Papilio indra
2.0-3.0″

BLACK SWALLOWTAIL

female

BAIRD'S SWALLOWTAIL
Papilio bairdi
3.3-3.5″

male

BLACK SWALLOWTAIL
larva and pupa

sagebrush. Like the adult, it varies in color but is usually green with a black stripe across each segment; on top are several yellow dots.

Perhaps the most common butterfly west of the Rockies, and one of the commonest of the swallowtails, is the Anise Swallowtail. It probably occurs so widely because of the abundance of its favorite food plant, anise or fennel, which is found in gardens and as a garden-escape west of the Rockies. This butterfly seems to delight in chasing other butterflies away from the hilltops and rocky crags that it likes so well. It may be seen in the southern part of its range from February to November and in the northern part of its range from May to July.

The Anise Swallowtail closely resembles the Alaskan Swallowtail. However, it generally has longer tails, less yellow dusting in the black parts near the base of the wings, and the orange spot at the margin of the hind wing is less conspicuous. The hornlike growths just back of the head of the Anise Swallowtail caterpillar are glands that are pushed out when the caterpillar is disturbed or irritated. They are harmless and appear to be only a protective device intended to frighten away other insects or animals that might be tempted to attack the caterpillars.

Another swallowtail species, the Indra Swallowtail, is also known as the Short-tailed Swallowtail. This butterfly has tails that may vary in length but which usually are short. The light markings are a creamy-yellow color instead of the bright yellow of the other swallowtails. The hind wing of this short-tailed swallowtail is pictured with that of the longer-tailed Black Swallowtail.

Although the Indra Swallowtail is seen at low altitudes early in the season, it prefers mountain tops. It seems to enjoy open, rocky summits and quickly drops over cliffs to slip away from any pursuer. Seldom does it pause in its swift, jerky flight to sip nectar from convenient flowers. This swallowtail is found on the high mountains of Colorado, Wyoming, Nevada, California, Oregon, and Washington.

male

SPICEBUSH SWALLOWTAIL
Papilio troilus
4.0-5.0″

hind wing
of female

SPICEBUSH larva

The Spicebush Swallowtail, another large species of swallowtail found in eastern United States, prefers the damp woods where its favorite food plants, spicebush and sassafras, grow. Its wings, like those of the Black Swallowtail, usually are kept in constant motion while it feeds. The males of the Spicebush Swallowtail give off the strongest scent of any of the swallowtail butterflies. It is said to be like the odor of certain brands of honey biscuits. The hind wings of the female are bluish instead of greenish as in the male. This is another one of the butterflies that produce exposures on film or photographic plates.

The dark-green caterpillar of the Spicebush

Swallowtail is called the "mellow bug." Behind the head are two pairs of eyespots, a conspicuous front pair and a small, buff-colored pair, each circled by a black ring. Viewed from the front, the caterpillar looks like a comic face. Before changing to the chrysalis, it becomes a dirty-yellow or dull-orange color. The chrysalis itself may be green, brownish or gray. Its smooth surface, with a distinct ridge running the entire length, distinguishes it from the other swallowtail chrysalids which have rough surfaces.

The Eastern Tiger Swallowtail occurs in a great variety of color forms, making it one of the most interesting and variable of all our butterflies. Certainly it is the most variable swallowtail. There are no less than 3 distinct forms of males and 11 forms of females. These butterflies vary from small, northern specimens to large, southern ones. Some males and females have bright-yellow wings crossed by

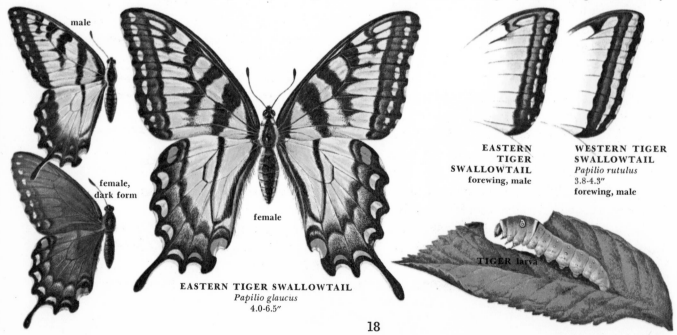

male

female,
dark form

female

EASTERN
TIGER
SWALLOWTAIL
forewing, male

WESTERN TIGER
SWALLOWTAIL
Papilio rutulus
3.8-4.3″
forewing, male

TIGER larva

EASTERN TIGER SWALLOWTAIL
Papilio glaucus
4.0-6.5″

18

black stripes and a black, yellow-striped band on the outer margin, or edge, of both the fore and hind wings. Other Tiger Swallowtails show all degrees of black in the wing scales. Some have so much black that the striped pattern is completely hidden. Intermediate forms between these extremes are common, but there is no relation between color, locality and season. Usually the females are larger and darker than the males.

The caterpillar has only a single pair of eyespots and does not show the color variation found in the adults. Its green color, lighter than the green of the Spicebush Swallowtail caterpillar, does not change to yellow or dull orange before it becomes a pupa. This caterpillar feeds on a wide variety of trees and shrubs but favors the tulip tree, ash and hop trees. It sometimes does considerable damage.

The Western Tiger Swallowtail looks like the Eastern Tiger except that it does not have as much color variation. Both males and females have similar color and markings. The underside of the fore wing has a yellow band along the edge instead of spots as in the eastern species. This butterfly is a familiar sight in the western states from spring until fall. It is easy to observe closely because of its lazy flight and frequent stops to sip nectar from flowers.

The finest looking butterfly of this group is the Two-tailed Swallowtail, another western species that prefers the semi-arid regions be-

tween the mountains for its home. Shadberry, prune, ash and privet are among the many trees and shrubs providing food for this most colorful of swallowtail caterpillars. The Pale Swallowtail or Mountain Swallowtail is also a western species. The markings are creamy white; the black bands are heavy.

The black-and-white banding on its wings gives the Zebra Swallowtail its name. An eastern species, it is most common in the south. The Zebra is one of the earliest swallowtails to appear and can be seen in the Middle Atlantic states by late March. Its favorite food plant is the pawpaw.

TWO-TAILED SWALLOWTAIL
Papilio multicaudata
4.0-5.3"
male

ZEBRA SWALLOWTAIL
Eurytides marcellus
3.8-4.5"
male

PALE SWALLOWTAIL
Papilio eurymedon
3.5-4.0"
male

ZEBRA SWALLOWTAIL larva

SMINTHEUS larva

male

SMINTHEUS
Parnassius smintheus
2.5-3.0"

CLODIUS
Parnassius clodius
2.5-3.0"

male

Parnassians

The second group of the papilio family, the parnassians, are strictly butterflies of the Northern Hemisphere. They often live in areas with a harsh climate. Only three species are recorded in North America, all in the northern or western part of the continent. Only one of these, Clodius, is limited to North America. The other two species also live in Asia and Europe. Parnassians are most common in the beautiful alpine meadows of the Cascade Mountains, on Vancouver Island in British Columbia, and even in the dry, inland areas of Oregon and Washington.

Clodius may be seen from California to southern Alaska, where it is frequently found at sea level in the spring. Later in the summer it is found in the Sierras and Cascade Mountains, eastward to the Rockies in Montana and Wyoming. Clodius is extremely variable; rarely are two specimens exactly the same. Some have much larger red spots on the hind wings than the specimen pictured. One rare variety occurs in a few isolated colonies along the coastal ranges of California. Because this butterfly is so typically an alpine species, it is surprising to find this one variety so far south

and at such a low altitude. This coastal form is much lighter than the typical form with very little of the blackish border on the fore wing. Other specimens have orange instead of red spots and very little black coloring at all. One species is limited to the basin of the Yukon River in North America. The male is a beautiful yellow; the female yellowish-white. This butterfly is similar in design to Clodius but is much smaller and its yellow ground color identifies it immediately.

Smintheus, sometimes called the Mountain Butterfly, is widely distributed in western North America. Some scientists consider this parnassian to be the same as the Asiatic and European species, which it closely resembles. In North America, Smintheus occurs in Alaska south of the Arctic Circle and as far south as the mountains of New Mexico, Colorado, Utah, and California. Like Clodius, this butterfly is extremely variable; many specimens have red or pink spots on the fore and hind wings.

The larvae of the parnassius butterflies are brownish, hairy caterpillars that feed on plants such as violets, sedum or saxifrage. The pupa is attached to an upright twig or to a blade of grass on the ground under dead leaves or grass. Parnassians hibernate, or rest, through the long winter in the pupal stage. In the spring the butterflies emerge and mate almost immediately—usually before the female's wings are fully dry and developed. At the time of mating, a peculiar pouch, which is characteristic of this group of butterflies, is formed at the end of the body of the female. Only mated females have this pouch; unmated females do not. The female lays her eggs one at a time and deposits them at random, not necessarily close to the food plant of the caterpillar.

Parnassians can fly rapidly when startled. They are found generally as constant visitors to flowers where they feed. They are sun-lovers and disappear immediately in the grass or under low plants when a cloud passes. On the ground their coloring conceals them.

Sulphurs and Whites

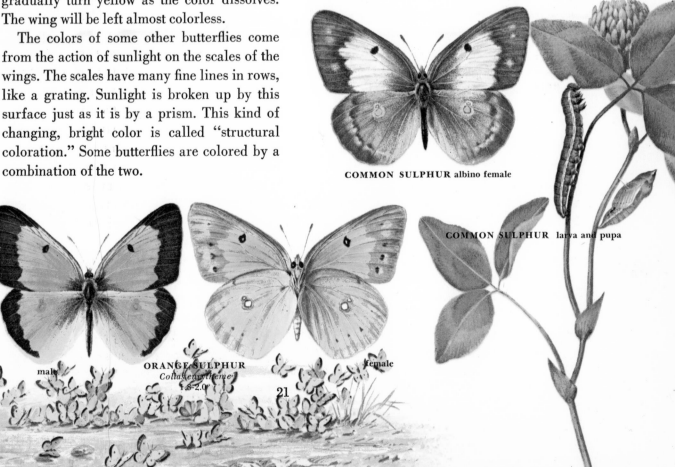

COMMON SULPHUR
Colias philodice
1.3-2.3″

In this large group are the bright-yellow butterflies that have given this entire group of insects their names. Many kinds are yellow as butter, so the name "butterfly" came naturally. The question of what makes them yellow, or what gives all butterflies their color, is an interesting one to explore.

The color of the scales of butterfly wings is produced in several ways. The scales on some butterfly wings are colored by chemical substances, or pigments. The yellow and white pigments of most sulphurs and whites are built up from a waste product within the insect. These sulfur colors are soluble in dilute ammonia, a fact which you can prove for yourself by placing a yellow butterfly wing in a white saucer. Add a tablespoon of water and household ammonia. Stir with a toothpick. The liquid will gradually turn yellow as the color dissolves. The wing will be left almost colorless.

The colors of some other butterflies come from the action of sunlight on the scales of the wings. The scales have many fine lines in rows, like a grating. Sunlight is broken up by this surface just as it is by a prism. This kind of changing, bright color is called "structural coloration." Some butterflies are colored by a combination of the two.

First in the group of sulphurs are the Orange Sulphur, or Alfalfa Butterfly, and the Common Sulphur. These are discussed together because their lives have become so mixed that sometimes it is impossible to tell one from the other.

A long time ago the Orange Sulphur lived in southern and western United States and the Common Sulphur lived in the eastern part. Gradually the Orange Sulphur spread to the East and then extended its range on into Canada. As it spread eastward, it mated with the Common Sulphur, which has produced all kinds of crosses, or hybrids. Because both species appear in several color forms, it is very difficult to determine to what species some

COMMON SULPHUR albino female

COMMON SULPHUR larva and pupa

ORANGE SULPHUR
Colias eurytheme
1.8-2.0″

male

female

21

color forms belong. Usually the males of the Orange and Common Sulphurs are like those pictured, but sometimes males of the Orange Sulphur show only a blotch of orange color in the wings. The females with pure yellow in the center of the wings are the Common Sulphurs and those with orange or part orange are the Orange Sulphurs. Both species have "white females," and it is difficult to assign any white female to one species or the other. Even butterfly experts are puzzled by the various forms of these two butterflies.

The grass-green, white-striped caterpillar of the Orange Sulphur feeds on alfalfa, but also likes lupine, vetch, clover, locoweed and other plants of the pea family. Sometimes the Orange Sulphur is a pest on alfalfa crops.

The Common Sulphur prefers white clover and thrives best on it. The caterpillar also eats other clovers, vetch, lupine and related plants. Both the Orange and the White Sulphurs usually hibernate as pupae, or chrysalids, but occasionally do so as larvae or adults.

It is interesting to note that the pupa is attached to its twig or food plant stem by means of a silken loop, as are the pupae of the other sulphurs and whites. This habit shows a relationship to the swallowtails. Generally the pupae of these butterflies have a conelike projection on the head, and sometimes the wing cases are greatly enlarged, forming a high ridge on the underside.

There are many kinds of closely related sulphurs throughout the Americas, Asia and Europe and a few in Africa. Most of them live in the northern parts of their range or occupy cooler areas at high altitudes in the southern parts of their range.

Not all of the species are yellow and black or orange and black in color. One, which occurs in the High Sierras of California, is green with black borders. Green coloring in butterflies is comparatively rare and a completely green butterfly—such as Behr's Sulphur—is extremely rare. Orange and Common Sulphurs

PINK-EDGED SULPHUR
Colias interior
1.3-2.0″

are fond of gathering together in great swarms on the damp earth around puddles or along streams, especially in hot, dry weather.

The male Pink-edged Sulphur has yellow wings with black borders, but in the female only the tip of the fore wing and a few marginal spots remain black. This butterfly was given its name because the narrow outer edges of both its fore and hind wings are bright pink. The Pink-edged Sulphur is a northern butterfly, common and widespread throughout its range. Another sulphur found in the Far North is the Hecla Sulphur, which lives in the arctic regions of both the New and Old Worlds. It is orange-colored, heavily dusted with brown and green scales above and below. The male's wings have black borders; the female's have yellow spots in the borders.

The orange tips and marbles are among the earliest butterflies to appear in the spring. Their bright coloring and delicate flight signal the end of winter. About a dozen species of these butterflies live in the United States but only one, the Olympia Marble, lives in the Middle West and the East. This butterfly does not have orange tips on the fore wings. On the underside of its hind wings are three uneven bands of green which look like the green running through a slab of marble. The Olympia Marble got its name from these. The green color is so intense that it shows through the upper surface of the wings.

The larva of the Olympia Marble is a striking green with stripes of gray and bright yellow running its entire length. It feeds on rock cress, winter cress, shepherd's purse, and other wild plants of the mustard family.

22

The first of the real orange tips is the Falcate Orange Tip, so called because the tips of the fore wings are shaped like a hook or sickle. It is the only one of the orange tips with this odd feature. Both male and female are white on top, but the male alone has orange tips on the fore wings. Only rarely does the female show a little yellow there. Both male and female are white underneath, with beautiful yellow-green marbling, especially on the hind wings.

The caterpillar of the Falcate Orange Tip, like that of the other orange tips, feeds on plants of the mustard family. It eats leaves, buds, flowers and seed pods. The coloring of the caterpillar is a dull green with fine stripes of blue, orange, white, pale yellow and olive.

The Falcate Orange Tip also spends the winter as a pupa. The butterfly emerges in March and spends its time flying leisurely about in open woodlands. Like other woodland species, it flies on cloudy as well as on sunny days. It prefers mountain valleys and ravines and occurs throughout the East, from Massachusetts to Illinois and Texas. In the North it has one brood a year, in the South, two broods.

The western orange tips are numerous as well as beautiful. The wing tips of the male are a vivid orange to a rich crimson color. The females rarely have the crimson tips but their wings may be deep yellow. This produces a beautiful contrast with the black borders and spots which they have at the ends of the cell area in the central part of the wing. Typical of this group is the Sara Orange Tip. The wings of this butterfly are normally white. In the male the deeply colored tip of the fore wing is set off by a black bar. The tip of the female's fore wing is paler and is generally broken up by black spots and a yellow bar. The undersides of the hind wings have a mottled appearance from the greenish-brown marbling there. Scientists have noted that there is less marbling in the second brood of the year than in the first brood. This may be caused by changes in moisture and in temperature (p. 27). Some of the females (about fifteen percent) are yellow. The rest of them are white.

There are several varieties of the Sara Orange Tip. Some are smaller than the one pictured; others are more yellow. Some have spots at the ends of the veins in the hind wings.

SARA ORANGE TIP
Anthocharis sara
1.0-1.3″

male

female

OLYMPIA MARBLE
Euchloe olympia
1.6-1.7″

male

FALCATE ORANGE TIP
Anthocharis midea
1.3-1.5″

male

female

OLYMPIA MARBLE
larva

The profile of a dog's face outlined on the fore wing gives the dog-face butterflies their name. Two kinds or species of these butterflies occur in the United States. One, the California Dog Face, is bright violet, yellow and black with a beautiful purplish sheen. The female differs from the male in having no dark color except a black spot on each of the clear yellow fore wings. The California Dog Face is also found in Mexico.

The second species is the Southern Dog Face, found east of the Rocky Mountains and south into Central America. Unlike the California Dog Face, the males and females are similar and do not show distinct differences. The caterpillar, like that of the California Dog Face, feeds on false indigo and clover. It is green, covered with small, black, bristle-bearing tubercles, or spikes.

Three of the many small sulphurs are shown in this book. These are the Fairy Yellow, the Dwarf Yellow and the Little Sulphur. They are thin-winged, feeble little butterflies which have a jerky, but sometimes swift, flight.

The Dwarf Yellow is a tiny butterfly found over most of the southern United States. A few females are completely white, others completely orange. The larva feeds on such plants as marigold, chickweed and sneezeweed. The Fairy Yellow ranges from South America to southeastern United States and into Texas.

The Little Sulphur is common and widespread over most of the eastern United States. This butterfly is noted for its migrations, and has been observed in enormous numbers far out at sea. In October, 1874, what was thought to be a cloud was seen approaching Bermuda. As it neared shore, it was soon seen that the "cloud" consisted of countless Little Sulphurs that had migrated a distance of 600 miles over the ocean.

No one knows where the Sleepy Sulphur got its name—certainly not because it moves slowly. When startled, it puts on a good burst of speed but otherwise it tends to flutter aim-

LITTLE SULPHUR
Eurema lisa
1.3-1.6"

male

FAIRY YELLOW
Eurema daira
1.0-1.3"

male

DWARF YELLOW
Nathalis iole
0.8-1.3"

male

SOUTHERN DOG FACE
Zerene caesonia
2.3-2.5"

male

LITTLE SULPHUR larva

LITTLE SULPHUR pupa

male

female

CALIFORNIA DOG FACE
Zerene eurydice
1.8-2.0"

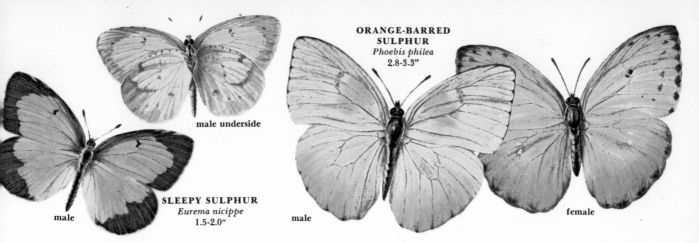

lessly. The Sleepy Sulphur, also one of the small sulphurs, is normally yellow, but is noted for its many color varieties. Some specimens are deep orange; others are white. Notice how the underside is different from the upperside. Like the Little Sulphur, the Sleepy Sulphur swarms; clouds of them may occasionally be seen in our southeastern states.

The giant or great sulphurs include brilliant species that are vigorous, rapid fliers. In flight, they stop frequently to sip nectar from flowers. Although the group is found mainly in New World tropical areas, several species are common in the southern parts of the United States, and occasionally toward the north.

The bright-yellow Cloudless or Senna Sulphur is found from South America north into California and into eastern United States. In the tropics these butterflies swarm in vast numbers to rest on damp ground along the edges of streams. This species too is famed for its

migrations and sometimes countless thousands will fly out to sea to certain death. The caterpillars of the Cloudless Sulphur are yellowish-green with a yellow stripe along each side and rows of black dots across each body section. The caterpillar of the Cloudless Sulphur is said to change to yellow when it feeds on the yellow flowers of its food plant and to green when it feeds on the leaves. This color change protects the caterpillar by making it difficult to see.

The Orange-barred or Red-barred Sulphur looks like the Cloudless Sulphur but is larger. Until the early part of this century, the Orange-barred Sulphur was found only in southern and central United States. Gradually it spread eastward to Florida and now strays are found as far north as Nebraska. The caterpillar is somewhat similar to that of the Cloudless Sulphur; both feed on cassia and related plants.

The Mustard or Veined White Butterfly is

25

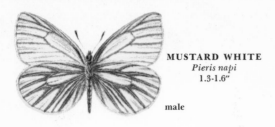

MUSTARD WHITE
Pieris napi
1.3-1.6″

male

almost pure white above but is colored along the veins on the underside. The brownish-green veins result from a close mingling of yellow and black scales.

Over a hundred years ago the Mustard White was a very common butterfly. Then a strange thing happened. The Cabbage White, which is not a native butterfly of this continent, was accidentally introduced into Quebec about 1860. From there it spread rapidly, and by 1881 it covered the eastern half of the continent. Two years later the first specimen was found in California. Now it covers almost all of the continent and does tremendous damage to cabbage.

As the Cabbage White spread, the native Mustard White disappeared and is now limited to a small part of its former range. Before the arrival of the Cabbage Butterfly, the larvae of the Mustard White probably fed on all cultivated and wild plants related to mustard and cabbage, but it was unable to compete with the Cabbage Butterfly. Now it seems to be limited to rock cress, water cress, and related wild plants. The Cabbage White prefers open spaces but is gradually invading woodlands.

One of the handsomest whites is the Pine White, commonly found in British Columbia, Washington and Oregon. Sometimes immense

numbers of these butterflies die after laying their eggs high in pine or fir trees. The dead butterflies cover the ground like drifted snow. The green-and-white caterpillars occasionally strip the leaves from whole forests of conifers on which they feed. The caterpillar forms its chrysalis in the crevices of the bark of conifers. Another species of Pine White lives in Mexico, Arizona and southern California. It has much more black on its fore wings.

The next three whites are similar to the large sulphurs in size and occupy much of the same area in the southern part of the United States. The Great Southern White is abundant in the southern part of its range. Sometimes great migrating masses are found along the Florida coasts. There are two forms of this butterfly. In one form, the females are like the males; in the second form, the females are dusky, contrasting with the white males. Scientists have shown that the dusky variation is associated with the migratory habit of this butterfly. Overcrowding often is one cause of migration, but there may be other causes, such as the gradual disappearance of the food plant or attacks by parasites. Not all of the populations of this butterfly migrate. The food supply of the Southern White, like those of many whites, covers a variety of plants related to cabbage and mustard. One unrelated plant, saltwort, is known to be eaten by the caterpillars of the Great Southern White. They eat this new source of food when their usual food plant is lacking and they are forced to migrate.

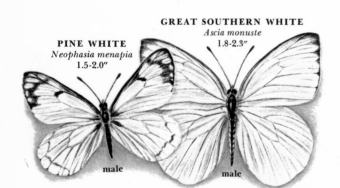

PINE WHITE
Neophasia menapia
1.5-2.0″

GREAT SOUTHERN WHITE
Ascia monuste
1.8-2.3″

male

male

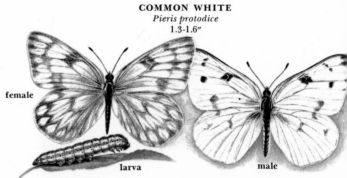

COMMON WHITE
Pieris protodice
1.3-1.6″

female

larva

male

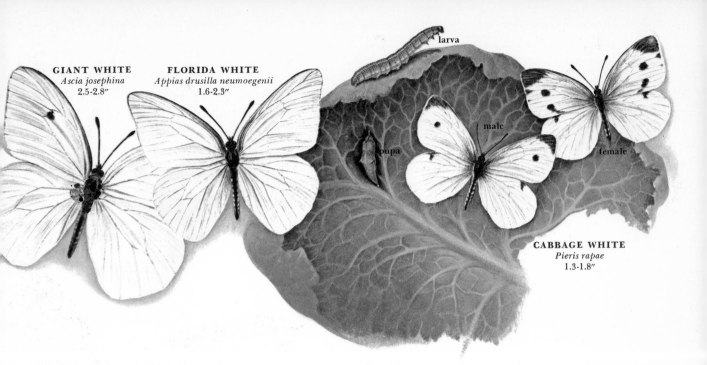

GIANT WHITE
Ascia josephina
2.5-2.8"

FLORIDA WHITE
Appias drusilla neumoegenii
1.6-2.3"

larva

pupa

male

female

CABBAGE WHITE
Pieris rapae
1.3-1.8"

The Giant White, a Central American species, is found in the Rio Grande Valley of Texas. It is the largest of our whites and, except for the black spot on the fore wing, it has no markings. Another characteristic of this species is that it has chalk-white scales along the veins on the upper surfaces of the wings.

The male Florida White is similar to the Giant White, except that it has no black spot in its fore wing. The females vary greatly in color and markings but, as in the male, there is always a spot of orange color on the underside at the base of the fore wing.

The Common White, found throughout the United States, is a good representative of this group of butterflies. Sometimes it is called the Checkered White because of the checkered pattern of the wings. Notice that the dark markings are much darker in the female than they are in the male.

At one time this butterfly was much more abundant than it is now, but that was before it had to enter into competition with the Cabbage White. The Common White prefers roadsides, waste areas, and other open places. Even when alarmed, it never darts into the woods to hide. Almost any plant related to cabbage, mustard or turnips is acceptable as food to the downy, yellow-and-purple-striped larva. One form of this Common White is darker and smaller than the usual specimens. It is found high above sea level. Its color and size are the direct result of a low-temperature environment.

Just what effect does temperature have on butterflies? It has a marked effect on the production of melanin, the pigment which causes the black and brownish colors. High temperatures slow down or prevent the production of melanin; low temperatures speed it up. Temperature could be responsible for the seasonal color variations so common in butterflies, but there is more to it than that. Sometimes the production of melanin in a species is controlled by inherited factors. For example, one would expect the generation of butterflies that spends the winter in low temperatures to be dark, but the reverse may also be true.

The flavones make up another group of pigments found in some sulphurs and whites and other butterflies. The flavones occur in whitish and yellow flowers that are eaten and eventually appear in the wings of the adult. When ammonia is dropped on the wing of a specimen the flavones produce a deep yellow color. This color does not last long. It soon fades and the original color of the wing returns.

Milkweed Butterflies

The milkweed butterflies belong to a family that is found widely throughout the world. One species, the famous Monarch, is perhaps the best-known butterfly in the United States. Milkweed butterflies are large and showy. They are also known for their long migrations. Their natural protection from other animals is so well established in the insect world that other butterflies, lacking this protection, mimic the milkweed butterflies and apparently secure the same results.

The richly colored Queen is found mainly in the southern states but occasionally it strays north into the Midwest. A form of the Queen, with white scales along the veins of the hind wings, is found in California. The caterpillar of the Queen is light brown, with narrow bands of brown and yellow across its body and with a yellow stripe along each side. It has fleshy spurs like the Monarch, and feeds on milkweeds. The female Queen produces three broods a year.

male

QUEEN
Anosia gilippus berenice
3.1-3.3"

male

MONARCH
Danaus plexippus
3.5-3.9"

MONARCH pupa

MONARCH larva

Both the Queen and the Monarch are "protected" species. This means that these butterflies are safe from attacks by birds and other insect-eating animals because the butterflies' bodies contain fluids that have an unpleasant taste. Just how enemies have learned to avoid these bad-tasting species is a biological puzzle—but the protection works. Although the Queen (and the Monarch) are able to fly for long periods of time, they have developed a leisurely, soaring flight because they have nothing to fear from predators. The butterflies that imitate them, such as the Viceroy, with no "built-in" protection of their own, have associated closely with the protected types and have come to look very much like them. Wherever the Queen is found, the Viceroy is dark colored and mimics the Queen. But, in the north, the Viceroy is light colored and mimics the Monarch which has the same general form and color pattern.

The Monarch is probably the most famous migratory butterfly. A native American butterfly, it is distributed widely over much of the world because of its wandering habits. Even though it has received help from ships and planes in its travels, the vast number of places where the Monarch is now found is truly amazing. Almost every year it is caught in Great Britain, where it was first sighted in 1876. The Monarch normally overwinters, or spends the winter, in the south. Because it cannot overwinter in Great Britain, it must travel there every year, under its own power or with help. It has alighted on ships many hundreds of miles at sea and, in this way, it has hitchhiked around the world. It has reached Hawaii and from there has traveled westward, gaining a foothold in Australia and spreading rapidly north and west to neighboring islands. To survive, this butterfly needs only a warm climate and a supply of milkweeds.

In the United States we have the best opportunity to observe the migratory habits of the Monarch. Every year in the fall, vast numbers

Monarchs migrating

of these butterflies fly south to spend the winter. Great swarms of these insects sometimes develop along the eastern and southern coasts of New England in September; somewhat later in New Jersey. The swarms are so large that when they alight on trees already bare, the trees look as though they have a new autumn foliage.

As winter approaches, the Monarchs continue a leisurely flight southward on what appear to be regular routes of migration along both the East and West coasts. In California, at Pacific Grove, and Point Lobos, just south of the Monterey Peninsula, and in Florida, there are regular "butterfly trees" which are visited every year by the Monarchs and which serve as winter resting places for them. On bright days during the winter some of the butterflies take lazy flights in the sunshine and then return to their resting places. Earlier generations of Monarchs may have left a scent or odor on these trees which is strong enough to attract later generations.

On each hind wing of the males of the Queen and the Monarch is a patch of scales that produce a distinctive odor. The male also has a cluster of hairs on each side of the last segment of the abdomen. These can be rubbed against the scent scales to spread the odor which is important in courtship. This same scent may attract migrants to the butterfly trees.

The Monarchs go north in the spring in smaller numbers, laying eggs along the way, until they have gone as far north as their range permits. There are many broods or generations each year.

PEARLY EYE pupa   PEARLY EYE larva

LITTLE WOOD SATYR
Megisto eurytus
1.8"

male underside

EYED BROWN
Satyrodes eurydice
1.8-2.0"

male

CREOLE PEARLY EYE
Enodia creola
1.6-2.0"

male

PEARLY EYE
Enodia portlandia
1.6-2.0"

male

Satyrs

Satyrs are mostly brown or brownish butterflies, although a few species in the United States may be brightly colored. These attractive insects have equally attractive names, such at Meadow-browns, Graylings, Satyrs and Wood Nymphs. On their wings they all have conspicuous eyespot markings. These are dark in the center with one or more light-colored rings around them.

Satyrs are found in open woods, in meadows fringed with trees and along roads edged with shrubbery. Many prefer to fly in the shade or in the early evening. Their flight is weak, jerky and dancing. When alarmed, they dodge through bushes and are soon lost to sight. Resting satyrs fold their fore wings between their hind wings. This exposes the shades and pro-

tective mottling and mingling of colors of the hind wings. The butterflies are then difficult to see. The satyrs have very small front legs. The male's are much smaller than the female's and have only one joint.

When first hatched from the egg, the caterpillar has a very large head and a small body. But after it has fed well on grasses and sedges, it becomes quite slender and tapers from the middle toward each end. The tail end of the caterpillar is forked, a feature that makes it different from nearly all other caterpillars. The chrysalis is a plain green or brown and usually may be found on the ground in debris or under rocks; sometimes it is found hanging by its tail from a twig.

The Eyed Brown, unlike most satyrs, favors open marshy areas. The caterpillar does not follow the usual habits of the family; it feeds by day instead of by night, as the others do. Although the typical Eyed Brown is a northern butterfly, varieties are found all the way south to northern Florida.

The Pearly Eye is a forest butterfly, living in open woods and forest edges. The males alight on tree trunks and adopt a "territory," as some birds do. They will chase all intruding butterflies from their "territory." Fights between males are common. They break out when one tries to protect his tree (to which he will return day after day) from being claimed by another.

The Creole Pearly Eye is another forest butterfly. It also claims a tree trunk as its territory and fights off other butterflies. It flies swiftly, usually in the shade, or at dusk, long after other butterflies have retired for the evening. The ranges of the Pearly Eye and Creole Pearly Eye are similar—from Manitoba to the Gulf states. But the Pearly Eye tends to be very local, with many miles separating the small, isolated colonies from each other.

The group to which the Wood Satyrs belong is extremely large. Most species are tropical, but six are found in the United States. All have typical satyr markings and are small- or medium-sized. They are brown or brownish in color and all have conspicuous eyespots on their wings. The Wood Satyrs are woodland species that prefer sunlit trails or open spaces in the forest. Occasionally they stray into open fields but only one species regularly frequents these clearings. The larvae of all the Wood Satyrs feed on grasses.

The Little Wood Satyr is found from southern Canada to Nebraska and south to the Gulf states and Florida. The adults are tricky to catch. They fly close to the ground, and then dart into a clump of bushes to emerge ten to fifteen feet away on the other side. The caterpillar is greenish-brown with a fine hairlike covering and narrow stripes running the length of the body. Its head and body spots are whitish.

The Gemmed Satyr is found from Illinois and Virginia to Florida and Mexico. The cater-pillar differs from most of the other satyrs—it is green in the early broods and brown in the later ones. In the warmer areas of its range, the Gemmed Satyr is reddish-brown and the dark lines are not as well marked as they are on the ones farther north.

One of the smallest species of this group is the Carolina Satyr. Its flight and habits are similar to those of the Little Wood Satyr but it is more common in damp or swampy woods. The Carolina Satyr is smaller and darker than the Little Wood Satyr.

The Georgia Satyr, unlike other satyrs, seems to prefer open marshes and bogs. Sometimes this butterfly frequents open pine woods and grassy areas.

Some butterflies have the same color and markings even when they are found over a wide geographic area. Others may vary according to region. One species may be darker in the south than in the north, or lighter in the east than in the west.

Any large collection of ringlets from various parts of North America will demonstrate this fact. The Plain Ringlet and California Ringlet are varieties or races of a single species. The same species occurs in North America, Asia and Europe. The illustrations show the extent of color variation due to geographic factors.

The larvae of the ringlets, like those of the satyrs, feed on grasses. The caterpillars are long and slender and have two short projections on the back end of their bodies.

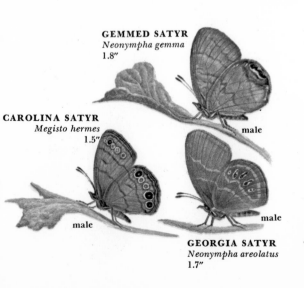

GEMMED SATYR
Neonympha gemma
1.8"

CAROLINA SATYR
Megisto hermes
1.5"

male

male

male

GEORGIA SATYR
Neonympha areolatus
1.7"

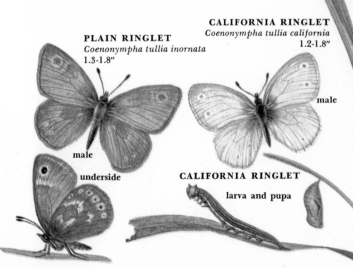

PLAIN RINGLET
Coenonympha tullia inornata
1.3-1.8"

CALIFORNIA RINGLET
Coenonympha tullia california
1.2-1.8"

male

male

underside

CALIFORNIA RINGLET
larva and pupa

The strikingly beautiful markings of the Riding Satyr of the Rocky Mountains distinguish it clearly from all the other satyrs. This grassland species is found as far west as eastern California.

The Wood Nymphs are medium-sized butterflies, velvety-brown or gray in color. Some have conspicuous yellow bands on the fore wings on which there are also eyespots with white centers. The flight of Wood Nymphs is jerky and darting. They have a habit of alighting on the ground or on tree trunks, and then closing their wings. In this position they are nearly invisible, because of the mottled coloring of their exposed under wings. The Wood Nymph larvae, like those of the satyrs, feed on grasses. The newly hatched fall larvae hibernate through the winter and resume feeding in the spring.

The alpines belong to a group of satyrs that are found mainly in the Far North. Only 10 species live in North America. Some occur in the southern parts of western mountains, but no alpines are found in eastern United States. The Common Alpine ranges from Alaska south along the Rocky Mountains into New Mexico. It is also found in the Cascade Mountains of Washington and Oregon. These pretty, rather dark-colored butterflies have a slow, wandering, soaring flight. They stop frequently to feed on the numerous alpine meadow flowers. When they are startled, however, as if they are waking from a dream, they take off swiftly and vigorously to escape from their pursuer.

The arctics, like the alpines, are found in the Far North or at high altitudes, chiefly in the mountains of western North America. A few invade the lowlands but they are the exceptions. These butterflies are adapted to life under severe climatic conditions of the north and of cold, windswept mountain tops. Although a species may be found over a wide area, nearly every mountain top where it occurs has its own small, distinctive population. Each population may show variation in color and form.

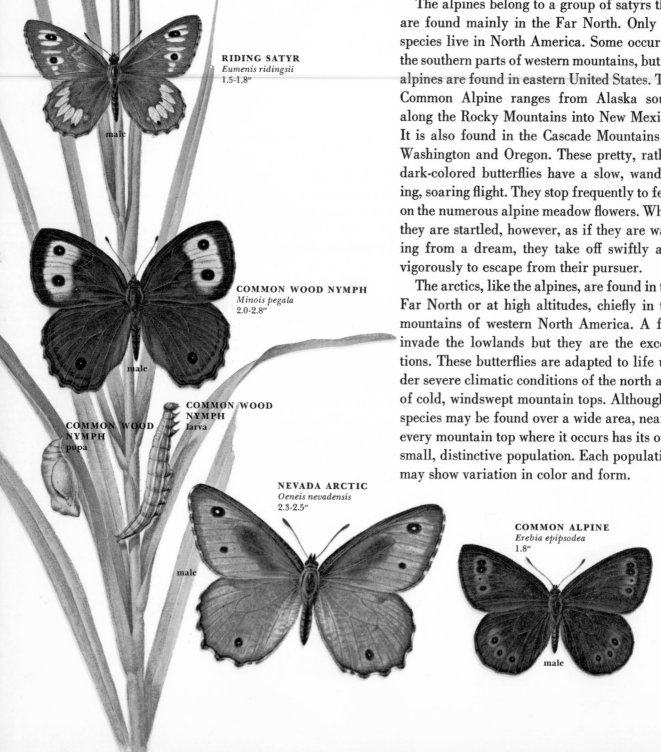

RIDING SATYR
Eumenis ridingsii
1.5-1.8"
male

COMMON WOOD NYMPH
Minois pegala
2.0-2.8"
male

COMMON WOOD NYMPH
larva

COMMON WOOD NYMPH
pupa

NEVADA ARCTIC
Oeneis nevadensis
2.3-2.5"
male

COMMON ALPINE
Erebia epipsodea
1.8"
male

Heliconians

The heliconians, or "long wings," are chiefly tropical butterflies, but a few species fly as far north as southern United States or even stray into the Midwest. They are medium- or large-sized, with brilliant colors and designs. These butterflies have such a variety of patterns and colors, and are so widely imitated by other butterflies, that they are an entomologist's nightmare.

The Zebra or Yellow-barred Heliconian and other members of this group are "protected" like the milkweed butterflies, probably because their body fluids make them unpleasant tasting to birds. One naturalist tried to urge a monkey, which was very fond of eating insects, to eat heliconians. The monkey showed his obvious dislike after he tasted them. Because they have this protective characteristic and live in the tropics where butterflies are abundant, heliconians are widely mimicked by other butterflies as well as by moths. Different heliconians also mimic each other.

The flight of the Zebra is most confusing as it flies along a sun-dappled forest trail. Its striped color pattern makes it nearly impossible to tell whether this butterfly is coming or going. Its food plant is the passion flower, a southern vine.

The Gulf Fritillary belongs with the Zebra although it looks quite different. It also resembles the true fritillaries (p. 34), but it has long, slender wings with brilliant, longish spots on the underside. This butterfly is common in the southern part of the United States but may be found as far north as Nebraska. Its larva feeds on the passion flower.

The Julia mimics the true heliconians, as is shown by its elongated wings. The real Julia is found in South America, but two races occur in the southern part of the United States. Its caterpillar, like the Zebra and the Gulf Fritillary larvae, has long branching spines on the back. It, too, feeds on passion flower.

GULF FRITILLARY
Agraulis vanillae
2.6-2.8"
male

JULIA
Dryas julia
3.2-3.8"
male

ZEBRA larva

ZEBRA pupa

ZEBRA
Heliconius charitonius
3.0-3.4"
male

33

Fritillaries

The fritillaries introduce the brush-footed butterflies, so called because their front legs are short and are often covered with bristly scales like a brush. These form the largest family of true butterflies, and include the checkerspots and crescents. The fritillaries include many familiar species and some of our commonest and most beautiful butterflies.

English scientists have reported interesting experiments on the ability of butterflies to distinguish among different colors. They used the Pearl-bordered Fritillary, a species similar to the Silver Bordered Fritillary in America. Photographs of the butterfly were cut out and colored bright blue, crimson, dull red, green, brown, yellow and also the butterfly's natural color—a tannish-yellow. The spots were black as in the living butterflies. These photographs were pinned to grasses where Pearl-bordered Fritillaries were flying. The tannish-yellow photographs attracted 27 live butterflies; the dull-red models attracted 18; and the yellow, 2. The bright-blue, green, brown and crimson models attracted no live butterflies at all.

In further experiments, scientists removed the color from dead specimens of the Pearl-bordered Fritillary. Then they colored some specimens with the same colors they used on the photographs. Two specimens of each color and two without any color were pinned to the grass. The live butterflies paid 13 visits to the two red specimens and the two yellow specimens and 13 visits to the two tannish-yellow specimens. They paid no attention to those dyed blue, green, brown or crimson. This is direct evidence that the Pearl-bordered Fritillary can distinguish color and suggests that the males may find the females by sight and not by scent.

The Variegated Fritillary is rare in New England but common south of Virginia into Central and South America. This fritillary is varied in color and markings. The caterpillar

VARIEGATED FRITILLARY
Euptoieta claudia
2.3"

male

REGAL FRITILLARY
pupa

male

REGAL FRITILLARY
Speyeria idalia
3.4-3.6"

34

larva

pupa

male

male underside

has six rows of spines that spread out like branches on its orange-red, brown-striped body. Violets and pansies are its favorite food, and sometimes the larvae are destructive in gardens and nurseries.

The true northern or greater fritillaries are medium to large in size, mostly orange-brown in color with black spots. On the undersides, especially on the hind wings, are uneven rows of silver spots. Sometimes these beautiful species are called Silver-spotted Fritillaries.

All these large fritillaries are strong, fast fliers but they stop frequently at flowers to feed. The caterpillars eat violets and feed only at night. During the daytime they hide, but not on the food plant.

The Great Spangled Fritillary is one of the most familiar eastern silverspots. Large in size and rich in color, it is one of our most attractive butterflies. It is often found in wet meadows and open woods from eastern Canada, west to Michigan and Oklahoma, and in the mountains south to Georgia. The males appear in May, the females about the first of June, and then both in increasing numbers until early sum-

mer. By the middle of August they start to disappear and by September they are scarce. The body of the larva, which is black, has six rows of black, branched spines marked with orange-red at their bases.

The Regal Fritillary, another large and attractive species, is well named. The males and females are similar in color. The rich blue-black hind wing distinguishes it from all of our other fritillaries. The male has a single row of cream-colored spots on the hind wing; the female has a double row. This butterfly likes open grassy meadows near wet or marshy places. Small isolated colonies occur from Maine to the Carolinas, westward to Nebraska and Arkansas.

The Aphrodite Fritillary (p. 36) is very much like the Great Spangled Fritillary but appears later in the season. This butterfly is varied in appearance. In some the black spots may become so enlarged that they merge with each other. Then the ground color of the wings, both above and below, may become hidden by dark scales. The caterpillar of the Aphrodite resembles that of the Great Spangled Fritillary except that it has a velvety-black spot on the base of each spine. The knobs on the back of the chrysalis, too, are shorter than those in the Great Spangled Fritillary. Aphrodite is common in northeastern United States, particularly in the mountains of New York, Pennsylvania and West Virginia. It likes marshy clearings, fields and open woods.

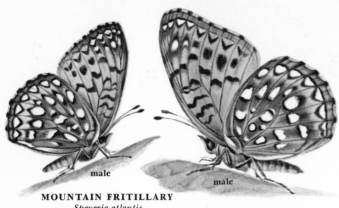

MOUNTAIN FRITILLARY
Speyeria atlantis
2.7-2.9″

APHRODITE FRITILLARY
Speyeria aphrodite
2.7-3.0″

DIANA FRITILLARY
Speyeria diana
3.7-3.8″

female

Another silverspot, the Mountain or Atlantis Fritillary, is frequently confused with the Aphrodite Fritillary. It is, however, smaller with narrower, darker wings. The Mountain Fritillary is found in the mountains along the Atlantic and Pacific oceans and in the highlands near the Great Lakes.

The grandest fritillary of all is the Diana. This large species is an unusual fritillary because of the marked difference in the coloring of the males and females. The female Diana has wings that are black at the base, like the male's, but are marked with blue toward the edges rather than with reddish-brown. It is said to mimic the Pipevine Swallowtail, which it does resemble. The unpleasant taste of this swallowtail protects it from attackers.

The Diana Fritillary is a shy, retiring butterfly. The males are generally found along woodland roads, but the females keep to woods and thickets and are difficult to catch. This cautious butterfly is seldom attracted to flowers but it does like manure piles. Although it has a rather wide distribution in eastern United States, it is rare except in a few widely scattered localities.

The Nevada Fritillary is another western species, found in the Rocky Mountains of Nevada, Utah, Montana and Canada. The ground color of this species, a pale yellow-brown, is not hidden by darker markings. The outer margins of the wings are black. On the underside, the fore wings are light tan with

DIANA FRITILLARY
Speyeria diana
3.7-3.8″

male

NEVADA FRITILLARY
Speyeria nevadensis
2.5-3.5″

male

EURYNOME SILVERSPOT
Speyeria eurynome
1.7-2.0″

male

silvery spots but the hind wings are green with brightly silvered spots. The Eurynome Silverspot is common in Colorado, Montana and Canada. It belongs to a puzzling group of several similar species that live in roughly the same area. Very little is known about the eggs and caterpillars of this group.

Lesser fritillaries include 16 or so species; all but 5 occur in Asia and Europe as well as in the United States. The lesser fritillaries are small- to medium-sized butterflies that are somewhat like the greater fritillaries and are sometimes included with them by the experts. These northern butterflies are found from the arctic tundra southward on mountain tops and in meadows and bogs. Almost nothing is known about the early stages of these handsome little butterflies.

The Eastern Meadow Fritillary differs from its close relative, the Western Meadow Fritillary, by having a narrow fore wing with a squarish tip. It is one of the greatest travelers among the lesser fritillaries. The Eastern Meadow Fritillary is found from British Columbia across Canada to eastern United States and in the Rocky Mountains southward to Colorado. It follows the eastern mountains to

North Carolina, and also occurs at low elevations in parts of the Midwest. Its larva feeds on violets and the butterfly seldom wanders from damp meadows or marshes where its food plant grows. The caterpillar is shiny green with a velvety-black stripe along each side and dull yellowish-brown knobs and spines.

The Silver Bordered Fritillary is present in much the same area as the Eastern Meadow Fritillary but it does not have that butterfly's "squared-off" tip on its fore wing. The Silver Bordered Fritillary, in a half dozen forms, is found in Europe as well as in the United States. This butterfly prefers marshes and wet meadows but occasionally strays to dry meadows and roadsides. The larva feeds on violets and one or two other plants. It is a spotty greenish-brown with barbed spines on the upper part of its body. Newly hatched or half-grown larvae hibernate and spend the winter in a resting state. The Western Meadow Fritillary is a common butterfly in the meadows of the Far Western states north to southern British Columbia and Montana.

Although all of these little butterflies are called fritillaries, they do not have the silver spots that are found in the greater fritillaries.

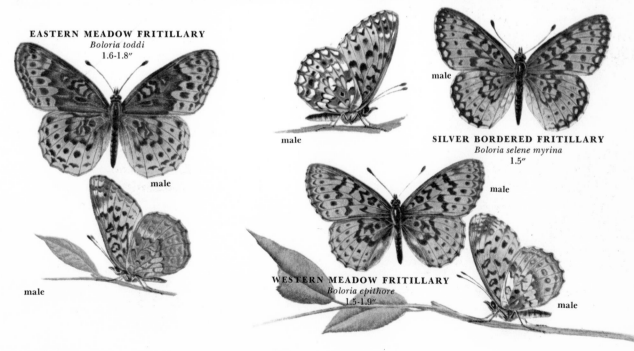

EASTERN MEADOW FRITILLARY
Boloria toddi
1.6-1.8"

male

male

male

SILVER BORDERED FRITILLARY
Boloria selene myrina
1.5"

male

male

WESTERN MEADOW FRITILLARY
Boloria epithore
1.5-1.9"

male

male

Checkerspots

Most of the checkerspots are western butterflies. They are often found in small, separated colonies. Frequently it is impossible to distinguish the species of these most attractive butterflies because they occur in a number of races, varieties and intermediate forms.

One of the largest of the checkerspots is the Baltimore, a wide-ranging eastern species. It is extremely local and is found only where its larval food plant, turtlehead, grows. Seldom does it wander more than a few yards away. Checkerspots are generally eager feeders but the Baltimore seldom visits the flowers of its food plant. The larvae of the Baltimore have a peculiar habit—all of them feed together in the same web. When autumn comes they hibernate in the web. In the spring they continue feeding until they become pupae. The pupa is grayish with dark brown stripes, dotted with a few orange-red spots. Usually the pupa is found hanging a considerable distance from the food plant.

The Silvery Checkerspot has a bright silvery crescent on the underside of the hind wing at the outer margin. It is a common butterfly that frequents lake shores, roadsides and open meadows in southern Canada and eastern United States, south to Georgia, and westward to the Rocky Mountains. The full-grown caterpillar is velvety-black with a dull orange stripe down the back and purplish bands on the sides. The body is covered with short, black spines. Various sunflowers, asters and related plants are eaten by the larvae.

Harris' Checkerspot covers much the same territory as the Silvery Checkerspot but goes a little farther north. A common white northern aster provides food for the larva. Another of the beautiful Far Western species is the Chalcedon Checkerspot. This checkerspot is a changing species; there are no two specimens absolutely alike.

BALTIMORE
Euphydryas phaeton
1.8-2.6"

male

BALTIMORE pupa

**SILVERY
CHECKERSPOT**
Melitaea nycteis
1.5-1.6"

HARRIS' CHECKERSPOT
Melitaea harrisii
1.4-1.7"

male

male

HARRIS' CHECKERSPOT

CHALCEDON CHECKERSPOT
Euphydryas chalcedona
1.8-3.0"

male

BALTIMORE larva

Crescents

The crescents are closely related to the checker-spots. In the United States these little butterflies are colored in quiet shades of brown, yellow and black. In the tropics numerous species imitate the "protected" heliconians (p. 33). Crescents are named for the crescent-shaped spot on the underside of the hind wing at the outer margin.

All of the crescents are eager feeders and visit flowers readily. Early in the morning before the sun has dried the dew, they like to rest on foliage with their wings open, warming themselves in the sunshine. If not disturbed, they will remain motionless for as much as an hour. The caterpillars are dark, marked with light stripes. The body is decorated with small bumps, arranged in regular rows. As far as is known, these caterpillars do not spin community webs at any time. The chrysalis always hangs with the notched, or divided, head down.

The Mylitta Crescent is a western species common in the Rocky Mountains, where its caterpillar feeds on thistle. The spines on this caterpillar differ from the other crescents. Most of their spines are black but on three segments, or sections, they are yellow.

The Field or Meadow Crescent is a medium-sized species with dark coloring on the upper-side of the wings. It ranges from Alaska to Arizona. The Phaon Crescent is found along the Gulf states to eastern California, and south to Guatemala and Cuba. The Pearl Crescent, one of our most familiar butterflies, is abundant from Canada to Mexico and is a frequent visitor to flowers and puddle edges. It is one of the small but warlike butterflies that seem to delight in chasing other species from its "territory." The coloring of the undersides of the wings of Pearl Crescents varies with the broods; the spring brood has darker markings resulting from the effect of cold on the over-wintering pupa. The summer brood has paler colors.

MYLITTA CRESCENT
Phyciodes mylitta
1.2-1.5"
male

male

FIELD CRESCENT
Phyciodes campestris
1.2-1.4"
male

PHAON CRESCENT
Phyciodes phaon
0.9-1.3"
male

PEARL CRESCENT
Phyciodes tharos
1.3-1.7"
male

female, dark phase

PEARL CRESCENT
larva and pupa

PEARL CRESCENT
female, bright phase

FLORIDA PURPLE WING
Eunica tatila
1.6-2.0"

Other Brush-Footed Butterflies

RUDDY DAGGER WING
Marpesia petreus
2.6-2.8"

On this page are some of the species of brush-footed butterflies that do not fall into one of the larger groups, such as the fritillaries, checker-spots and crescents. The Purple Wings live in the tropics. Over 60 species are found in tropical America but only a few reach our southern boundaries. Their coloring is brilliant and iridescent. The iridescence is caused by white light breaking up into a play of colors as it strikes microscopic striations or lines on the wing scales. The Florida Purple Wing is one of two species that are found in that state. It is limited to the shady hardwood forest or hummocks. It habitually alights on tree trunks where its mottled underside affords it protective concealment.

About 24 species of dagger wings are found in the American tropics but only 3 of them reach the more southern parts of Florida and Texas. The Ruddy Dagger Wing is probably the best known in the United States. It is found in Florida and Texas.

MIMIC
Hypolimnas misippus
2.5-3.0"

The tropic queens, a group which includes a large number of species, reach their greatest development in the Old World tropics. These species are among the most beautiful and the most unusual forms that mimic the "protected" milkweed butterflies. The beautiful Mimic is an Old World species that has found a home in the New World. It is unusual because the appearance of the male differs so greatly from that of the female. The uppersides of the male's wings are velvety-black with large white spots that reflect an iridescent purple. The female mimics several oriental species of milkweed butterflies. The female's color and pattern vary according to the species it mimics.

male

MIMIC

female

Angle Wings

These raggedy-edged butterflies form a group that is appropriately named "angle wings." The various species have distinctive names based on their markings and appearance. All of these butterflies have the tawny uppersides of their wings marked and spotted with brown or black. The undersides of the wings blend with the rough bark of trees, and often have a silvery mark like a comma or a "c."

The Question Mark has the silvery sign of the question on the underside of the fore wing. This is the largest of our angle wings and one of the earliest to appear in the spring. It hibernates as an adult. The caterpillar feeds on nettle, elm and hops.

The Satyr is a western butterfly. Its larvae feed on nettle. Like other angle wings, it has a "flash coloring" which gives it a certain amount of protection. In flight it "flashes" the bright color of its upper surface, which disappears when it alights. The butterfly may rest on bark or on the ground with the wings held straight up over the back. In this position it is practically invisible.

The Comma is also known as the "hop merchant." The Comma feeds on hops but its name comes from a superstition about the chrysalis. Along the back of the chrysalis are rows of small bumps that shine like metal. According to legend, the price of hops will be high if the spots shine like gold, but if they shine like silver, the price will be low. When the caterpillar is a little more than half grown, it cuts the veins of the hop leaf near the midrib and draws the edges of the leaf together to build a protected retreat while it is eating.

The Fawn feeds on willow, birch, alder and currant. The larva of the Zephyr feeds on azalea. Like the Zephyr, the Silenus angle wing is a western species.

41

QUESTION MARK
Polygonia interrogationis
2.5-2.8″

QUESTION MARK
male

male

QUESTION MARK
larva

QUESTION MARK
pupa

SATYR ANGLE WING
Polygonia satyrus
1.8-2.0″

male

male

COMMA
Polygonia comma
1.8-2.0″

COMMA
larva

COMMA
male

COMMA
pupa

larva

pupa

BUCKEYE
Junonia evarete coenia
2.0-2.3"

Buckeyes

Fewer than 20 species of the buckeyes or "peacock butterflies" are known and only three of them occur in the United States. The most common species is found through most of eastern and southern United States westward to California.

This species has been the subject of considerable experimentation. By mating selected pairs of progeny of a single female and then crossing those examples with the desired qualities, color changes can be gradually brought about. By rearing the caterpillars under moist, warm conditions, the ground color produced is darker and the eye spots are larger. By cooling

the caterpillars, striking changes in color and markings can be produced. A dry, warm environment tends to produce lighter colored butterflies.

Much of the life cycle of the Buckeye is pictured here. Butterflies and moths begin life as eggs. Usually the egg is deposited on or near the food plant, in case of the Buckeye, plantain, stonecrop, monkey flower, passion flower or snapdragon.

After hatching, the young larva feeds. As it gains in size it outgrows its skin. Then it sheds its skin or molts. The larva does this by attaching itself to a twig or leaf and remaining quiet for a time during which internal changes take place. After the quiet period, the skin splits from head to tail and the larva crawls out with a new skin. Every bump or spine comes out as if it had been cast in a mold. Usually there are four molts at fairly regular intervals. In some arctic species, which go into long hibernation under winter snows, the period of growth may take several years.

When the larva has finished feeding, it gets ready to form a pupa by attaching its tail to a small pad of silk which it spins onto a twig or leaf for support. Hanging head down for a day or two, the larva gradually twists itself into the form of the letter "J." Then its skin splits along the back and the pupa appears. By wriggling, the pupa works out of the cast-off skin as far as the tail. Finally, it pulls its tail from the skin and attaches it to the silken pad. Many butterflies remain in the chrysalis stage only a few weeks, but some species overwinter as pupae. When the stage of development in the chrysalis is well advanced, and the adult is ready to emerge, the front sections of the pupa split and out crawls the butterfly. This newcomer is still more or less wormlike and does not at first display the beauty of the fully developed insect. At first the wings are soft and shapeless. Then body fluids are pumped into them and within an hour or so they harden. The perfect butterfly is then ready to take off in flight.

Thistle Butterflies

The Painted Lady is sometimes called a cosmopolite, which means that it is found everywhere. It is probably the most widespread butterfly known. This butterfly is found wherever thistles grow: all over Europe and Asia; in Africa, except in the dense jungles; everywhere in North America except in the Arctic; throughout South America; in Australia and on many of the Pacific islands. Its larva feeds on many kinds of plants related to thistle—everlasting, sunflower, burdock, groundsel and sagebrush—but also eats hollyhock and other plants. The caterpillar lives alone in a nest made of silk, leaves, plant fragments and buds—a safe hideaway when it is not eating.

The West Coast Lady is the closest relative of the Painted Lady. Its range is not as great, extending from Vancouver Island in British Columbia to Argentina and (in the United States) as far east as Utah. The caterpillars are blackish, marked with interrupted orange lines and black spines. They prefer plants of the hollyhock family, which includes the hibiscus and mallow, but will eat privet and tree lupine. Some beautiful varieties of this butterfly do not have the black bars that normally cross the fore wings. This makes the butterfly much brighter. In another form, all the reddish-orange coloring on the wings has been replaced by a dirty white.

The Painted Lady probably migrates more than any other butterfly. Its migration is not like that of the Monarch, which flies south in the winter and north in the spring. The migration of the Painted Lady is of a type peculiar to several North American butterflies that are able to overwinter in the north. It is not a response to an instinct that causes a search for a

PAINTED LADY
Vanessa cardui
2.0-2.3"

male

male

male

WEST COAST LADY
Vanessa caryae
2.0"

male

male

warmer winter climate. It is a response to a scarcity of the food plant or to overcrowding. Such overcrowding may be caused by the absence of parasites or other enemies that prey on the Painted Lady and in this way keep the population down. This migration is not a yearly event, as with the Monarch, but occurs only at infrequent intervals. The West Coast Lady's migration is also of this type.

The Painted Lady was the species involved in the great migration of 1924, perhaps the largest migration ever recorded for a butterfly. This migration extended over 1,000 miles from the southern coast of California to the southern part of Colorado, and produced swarms of caterpillars that ate all available foods in some areas. This forced the next generation of butterflies to fly north in search of food, because the larvae had eaten all of the normal food plants. Later broods of caterpillars had to eat any food they could find and were reported doing damage to gardens and cultivated fields.

Another important migration of the Painted Lady took place in 1901. This one began in Lower California and lasted 11 days, covering the whole southwestern part of California. Months later, the part of Canada just north of the United States and east of the Rocky Mountains was full of these butterflies. They had covered a distance of 1,400 miles, and it is estimated that they moved at a rate of about 8 miles an hour.

The Painted Lady and the Red Admiral are common species in the British Isles. However, like the Monarch they make repeated migrations from the mainland. A few Red Admirals are able to withstand the cold and overwinter in Great Britain, but if it were not for repeated migrations, they would rapidly become extinct in the British Isles.

The American Painted Lady or Hunter's Butterfly is very similar to the Painted Lady and the West Coast Lady and is another wide-ranging butterfly. Its larva also likes plants related to thistle, especially the everlasting. The velvety-black caterpillar with yellow bands, white spots and black spines lives alone in a nest, like the Painted Lady caterpillar. It hibernates either as a pupa or as an adult.

The common and familiar Red Admiral is another wide-ranging thistle butterfly, found over most of North America, northern Asia, Europe, and Africa. It has also been introduced into New Zealand. The Red Admiral can be identified immediately. Against the nearly black ground color of its wings is a crossband of orange-red on each fore wing and a similar crossband around the margin of each hind wing, with white spots near the tips of the fore wings.

The Red Admiral hibernates as a pupa or adult and may be seen on the wing most of the year, weather permitting. It is found at all altitudes, from sea level to mountain top. The caterpillars are black, greenish, brown or a mottled white with black spines. They feed on nettles, hops and one or two other plants, and build a nest by folding leaves together. Each lives alone in this protective covering.

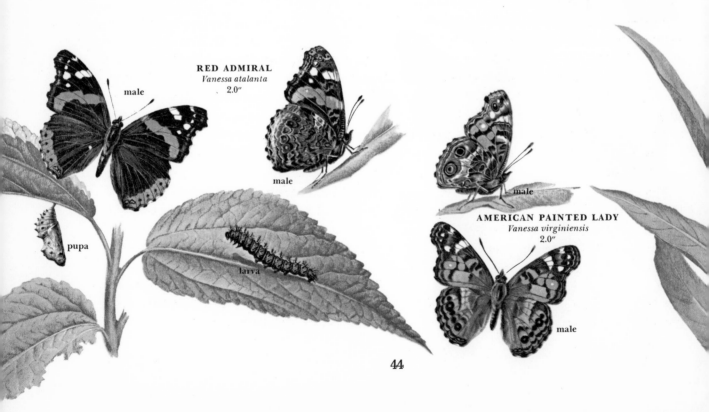

male

RED ADMIRAL
Vanessa atalanta
2.0″

male

pupa

larva

male

AMERICAN PAINTED LADY
Vanessa virginiensis
2.0″

male

Tortoise Shell Butterflies

These medium-sized butterflies are usually brown or black, marked with red, yellow or orange. The Compton Tortoise Shell is similar to the angle wing in coloring and the shape of the wings. It differs in having a straight lower edge to the fore wing and a white spot on each wing. The undersides of the wings are mottled, too, like the angle wings'. This butterfly is not called a tortoise because it is slow but because its rich brown and black markings look like the colors in polished tortoise shell. Although not a common butterfly, it is found in eastern United States, south to the Carolinas and Mis-

souri, and westward to Iowa, Washington, and Canada. The Compton Tortoise Shell is swift in flight. It folds its wings above its back and the exposed, marbled undersides mimic bark or dead leaves perfectly.

Milbert's Tortoise Shell or American Tortoise Shell is smaller than most of its relatives. It is easily recognized; it is blackish with an orange-brown band across its wings. Around the margins of the hind wings are small, blue crescent-shaped markings. This butterfly likes the mountains, but in the more northern parts of its range frequently moves into the lowlands. The larvae feed mostly on nettles but will sometimes eat willow or sunflower.

Interesting experiments on the color vision of butterflies have been made with the Small Tortoise Shell, closely related to Milbert's Tortoise Shell. A record was kept of the number of times the butterfly visited various white, pink and purple flowers. Of the more than 425 visits that were recorded, over half were made to purple flowers. Pink came next and less than 50 visits were made to white flowers.

In another experiment, transparent yellow, blue and red dyes were applied to the eyes of the Small Tortoise Shell. These colors did not affect the butterfly's movements. But if they had been blind to one of the dyes it would have had the same effect as black. When a black dye was used, the butterflies were blinded and were unable to fly or to control their flight. Other experiments show that color vision is not the same in all species of butterflies.

One of our most beautiful butterflies is the Mourning Cloak, or Camberwell Beauty. The rich, velvety, purple-brown wings with the broad yellow band on the outer margin and the row of violet-blue spots just inside present a striking color combination unlike anything else in the butterfly world. It is one of the most common and familiar species. The Mourning Cloak ranges over a wide area in Europe, Asia and North America. The larva feeds mainly on willow.

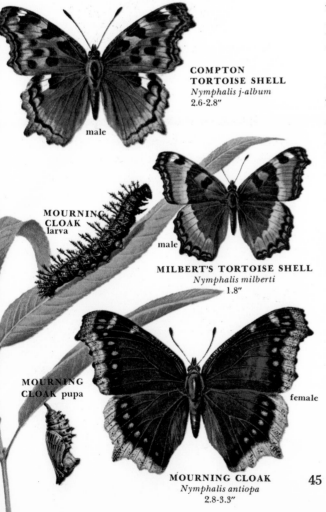

COMPTON TORTOISE SHELL
Nymphalis j-album
2.6-2.8"
male

MOURNING CLOAK larva

MILBERT'S TORTOISE SHELL
Nymphalis milberti
1.8"
male

MOURNING CLOAK pupa

female

MOURNING CLOAK
Nymphalis antiopa
2.8-3.3"

45

Viceroys
and Admirals

WEIDEMEYER'S ADMIRAL
Limenitis weidemeyerii
3.0″

male

LORQUIN'S ADMIRAL
Limenitis lorquini
2.3-2.8″

male

RED-SPOTTED PURPLE
Limenitis arthemis
3.1-3.4″

male

The Wiedemeyer's Admiral, common in the Rocky Mountains, does stray westward. For some unknown reason, this mountain butterfly has not been able to establish itself in the High Sierras of California where many conditions are favorable. This handsome admiral prefers damp places where its food plants, willow, aspen and cottonwood, are plentiful. The butterfly is identified by a series of white spots along the margin of its fore wing.

Lorquin's Admiral, the species of admiral best known on the West Coast, is easily distinguished from other admirals by the orange-red tips of the fore wing. The band on its wings is white with a slight buff tinge. In the more northern parts of its range, on Vancouver Island in British Columbia, the orange-red tips may be very small or may disappear completely. This may be the result of the cooler temperatures of the north. This species has a manner of flight typical of all the admirals— several twitching wingbeats are followed by a glide with the wings stretched out to the side.

The White Admiral is strikingly like the other two admirals, with white bands on its wings and a row of red spots with blue borders on the hind wing. This is also a northern butterfly, but it does not stray very far west in the United States or Canada. The White Admiral frequents open forests of birch, poplar, and willow, or clearings along the forest edge. A strong flier, like Lorquin's Admiral, it also stops frequently on a favorite perch high in some tree. It is fond of the sweet "honeydew" juices produced by aphids.

The Red-spotted Purple is now regarded as just a subspecies of the White Admiral, although it was once considered a distinct spe-

cies. It lacks the white bands which are so conspicuous on the White Admiral. The range of the Red-spotted Purple is more southern than that of the White Admiral. It takes over where the latter stops. This butterfly is as strong a flier as the White Admiral, but does not fly so high and frequently visits flowers.

Many plants provide food for the caterpillars of the Red-spotted Purple, among them, willow, poplar, wild cherry, hawthorn and birch. The caterpillars of this group of butterflies have an especially interesting feature. The egg is laid on the tip of a leaf of the food plant. The infant caterpillar begins feeding across the end of the leaf but does not touch the rib in the middle of the leaf. The larva feeds only at night; during the day it lies quietly, flat against the midrib, which it has previously prepared with a covering of silk and small fragments of the leaf. As the larva grows, it puts together a bundle of bits of leaf and silk. This bundle is fastened to the midrib next to the uneaten portion of the leaf. As the caterpillar feeds, it moves this bundle along the leaf.

When it has grown to about one-third of its full size, the caterpillar selects a leaf and eats almost the outer third of it. Then the larva binds the stem of the leaf to the twig so that the leaf will not fall off during winter storms, as it normally would. The caterpillar then draws the remaining part of the leaf together lengthwise and lines it with silk to form a tube. This is the winter home of the caterpillar and when completed it is just big enough to hold the caterpillar snugly. The larva crawls in head first and closes the tube with the back part of its body.

Some of these Red-spotted Purples have two or three broods. How does the caterpillar of the late brood or broods know how and where to make this winter home? After all, the home is built during the warm summer before there is any suggestion of winter weather, and there were no such winter homes built by the earlier brood. No one knows why some butterfly species have several broods or why some go into a resting period during the winter and some do not.

The caterpillars of the admirals can only be described as weird looking. They are greenish or olive-brown and their bodies are mottled and covered with warts and small lumps. The head has two lobes, or bumps, and behind the head rise a pair of large, rough, fleshy horns. The chrysalis is of uneven shape, with hollowed-out wing cases and a prominent hump.

The red-brown Viceroy, best known of all butterflies that mimic another, is completely different in coloring from the other members of this group. This butterfly mimics the Monarch—one of those butterflies having a nasty taste—apparently in order to protect itself from attack. The Viceroy ranges from central Canada south to Florida and Texas and into Mexico, where it is common in open places and along roadsides. Its flight is similar to that of its relatives, so it does not act like the Monarch when on the wing. The Viceroy's wings are held in the horizontal position typical of the admirals while gliding, while the wings of the Monarch are angled upward. The Viceroy also occurs in a great variety of forms and some of them look even more like the Monarch than the one shown. It is very fond of flowers and stops frequently to sip their nectar and the sweet "honeydew" juices on leaves.

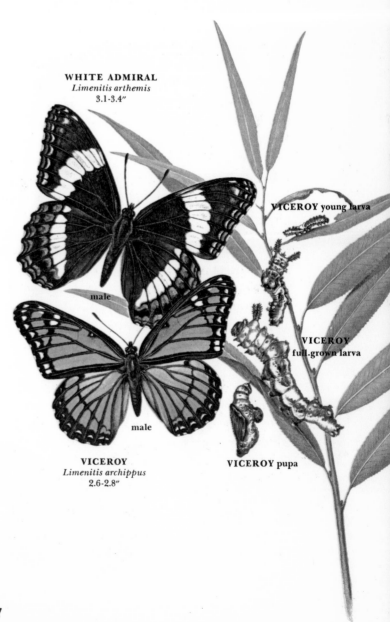

WHITE ADMIRAL
Limenitis arthemis
3.1-3.4"

male

VICEROY young larva

VICEROY
full-grown larva

male

VICEROY
Limenitis archippus
2.6-2.8"

VICEROY pupa

The California Sister, closely related to the admirals, can be recognized by the large orange-red spots of the fore wing. Lorquin's Admiral has similar spots but it does not have the blue lines on the undersides of the wings. The California Sister, in one form or another, is present from Mexico to the southern part of Washington, wherever the western live oak and Garry oak grow. It spends much of its time in solitary flight or perched on a high branch with outstretched wings, sunning itself. Like the admirals, its flight has a twitching motion followed by a glide in which the wings are held horizontally.

Experts who have studied this group of butterflies believe that the similarity between the California Sister and Lorquin's Admiral represents another case of mimicry, but there is no evidence to support the view that the California Sister could benefit as a mimic.

The early life stages of the Sister are quite

CALIFORNIA SISTER
Adelpha bredowii
2.5-3.0″

male

similar to those of the admirals and show clearly the close relationship between the two. The full-grown caterpillar is dark green on top with light-colored sides shading into brown below. The horns and spiky knobs are similar to those of the admirals but the coloring matches the color and texture of the oak leaves on which the larva feeds. Because of this color matching it is extremely difficult to observe. The chrysalis is brown with dark stripes and has a few metal-colored spots on the back.

Leafwing Butterflies

The Goatweed and Morrison's Goatweed are the only leafwings found north of Mexico. One species lives in Texas; the other gets as far north as Michigan. The entire group of leafwings has been well named—especially the larger tropical species. The upper surfaces of their wings are sometimes orange-red, sometimes brown or blue. The undersides are the color of dead

MORRISON'S GOATWEED
Anaea aidea morrisoni
1.9-2.2″

male

GOATWEED
Anaea aidea
1.9-2.2″

female

leaves. The tip of the fore wing is pointed and the edge of the hind wing has a sharp tail. When the butterfly alights on a tree and closes its wings, it looks like a dead leaf. This is another case of protective mimicry. These butterflies also have the added advantage of "flash colors." As they dart from or to their resting place, they display a flash of brilliant color, which disappears when they close their wings. The leafwing butterflies occur in two forms, a "dry season" form and a "wet season" form. The two forms often differ in color and in the shape of the wings.

In the early stages, the larva acts like the larvae of the admirals. After the third molt, it builds a nest by drawing the edges of a leaf of the food plant together lengthwise. By day it stays in this nest, crawling out at dusk to feed.

Emperor or Hackberry Butterflies

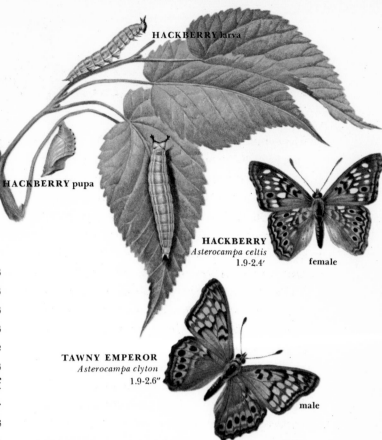

HACKBERRY larva

HACKBERRY pupa

HACKBERRY
Asterocampa celtis
1.9-2.4′

female

TAWNY EMPEROR
Asterocampa clyton
1.9-2.6″

male

These small butterflies take one of their names from their food plant, hackberry. The adults are yellowish or brownish with darker spots and bands across the wings. There are eyespots on the hind wings and in some species these are found on the fore wings also. The fore wings of the males are pointed and narrow; those of the females are broad and rounded. The hackberry butterflies are darting, vigorous fliers and often alight on tree trunks. They also sometimes alight on people.

The Hackberry or Gray Emperor is commonly found east of the Rocky Mountains but never reaches the Pacific slope. Some varieties have a few eyespots on their fore wings. The head of the caterpillar is squarish and is armed with a pair of sturdy, branching barbed spines. The body is shaped like a cylinder, sloping toward each end, with a divided, forklike tail. It looks rather like some of the caterpillars of the satyrs. The Hackberry larva hibernates when it is halfgrown.

The Tawny Emperor is like the Hackberry butterfly in many ways and the larva feeds on the same food plant. The adult has tawny, or yellow-brown, wings marked with black. Eyespots occur inside the margins of the hind wings but there are no eyespots on the fore wings. The larva is striped with green, yellow and white. It has the usual spines on the head and a forked tail. When young, the larvae live together in clusters. This caterpillar, like that of the Gray Emperor, hibernates when it is half-grown.

Butterflies are often attacked by animals or other insects that prey upon them. They face a much greater danger, however, from parasites —insects that attach themselves to the egg or caterpillar and eat it. The caterpillar is attacked by such parasites as tachinids, small flies and tiny, slender, wasp-like insects. Chalcids attack the eggs. Imagine how tiny this insect must be to be able to get all the food it needs for life from one butterfly egg!

The adult female of a wasp-like insect finds a caterpillar and lays an egg on it. When the egg of the parasite hatches, the larva eats its way into the living caterpillar. The caterpillar may live long enough to form a chrysalis but from it will come an adult of the wasp-like insect, not a butterfly. If the caterpillar dies before it can form a pupa, the parasite may form its pupa inside the skin of the dead caterpillar or it may fall to the ground to pupate. Often these parasitic insects can be useful. They are even imported into the United States and raised here to control destructive insects which are harmful to crops.

Metalmarks

MORMON METALMARK
Apodemia mormo mormo
1-1"

male

dark

NAIS METALMARK
Apodemia nais
1.0-1.3"

male

male

light

male

male

The name of these butterflies comes from the spots or lines on their wings that look like metal. Metalmarks are small butterflies and seldom have a wingspread of more than an inch. There are hundreds of species in the tropics, with every kind of pattern, wing shape and color combination. In the United States they are modestly colored. Although many kinds of metalmarks may be seen, there are not many individuals of any particular species. The males have only four walking feet but the females have six.

The Mormon Metalmark is a western species that occurs northward from Arizona and New Mexico, east of the Cascade Mountains, into north-central Washington. This attractive butterfly is ash gray and red, marked with white spots. Several varieties are found in the deserts of Arizona and California. The eggs are pink but just before hatching they turn violet. The larvae are short, thick and covered with bristly "hairs" (setae), some of which are very long and are bent downward. The short, plump pupa hangs by its rear end. It is held in place with a loop of silk, similar to that of the swallowtails, but pointing downward instead of upward.

The Nais Metalmark is the only metalmark in which the front legs of the male are well developed. The coppery-red wings are marked with dark brown and white and the edges are checkered. The pale green egg is shaped like a turban and is covered with a network of fine ridges. The caterpillar, yellowish-white and mouse-gray, differs from most caterpillars because the first section of its body comes up over its head, giving it a humped-up appearance. It feeds on wild plum. The chrysalis is blackish-brown. Like that of the Mormon Metalmark, it hangs by its tail and is held in place by a silken loop. The Nais Metalmark is found east of the Rocky Mountains from Colorado to Mexico.

The Little Metalmark is a common southern species, frequenting open fields and wet meadows from Florida to Virginia and west to Ohio, but it is rare in the north. This tiny butterfly is reddish-brown on top and brighter red on the underside. Both sides of the wings are covered with steel-blue, metallic spots arranged in rows. Nothing is known about its early stages.

The Swamp Metalmark did not even have a name until about 25 years ago because it had been confused with the Northern Metalmark. It feeds on swamp thistle and lives in swampy places, mostly in midwestern United States, wherever its food plant grows.

The Northern Metalmark is limited to the northeastern part of the United States, from southern New England to Virginia and Ohio. This butterfly prefers dry, hilly fields and open woods where its food plant, groundsel or ragwort, grows.

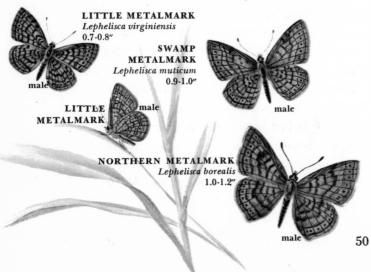

LITTLE METALMARK
Lephelisca virginiensis
0.7-0.8"

**SWAMP
METALMARK**
Lephelisca muticum
0.9-1.0"

male

**LITTLE
METALMARK**

male

male

NORTHERN METALMARK
Lephelisca borealis
1.0-1.2"

male

50

Snouts

COMMON SNOUT
Libytheana bachmanii
1.8-2.0"

Many fossil remains of insects have been discovered in recent years, particularly in the newly discovered fossil amber deposits of the Far North, Mexico, the Dominican Republic and elsewhere. Certain localities in America and Europe are rich in these remains. Some of these fossil insects are very closely related to kinds that exist today. This proves beyond a doubt that some of our insect groups have very ancient beginnings.

Fossil butterflies are not common, but a few examples belonging to the family containing the angle wings, admirals, silverspots and crescents have been found. Also some specimens of the satyr, swallowtail, sulphur and skipper families have been brought to light by men who study fossils. The species of satyrs found in deposits in France are more nearly related to those now found in America and India than to those of modern Europe. Most of the butterflies which have been found in the fossil state show a closer relationship to the butterflies now existing in the warmer parts of the earth than they do to those of the cooler regions.

Even though the fossils were formed about 20 million years ago, little change has taken place in the actual structure of butterflies. Most fossils of insects consist of the imprint of a wing or wings, sometimes a leg or two, a few fragments, or perhaps part of the body with legs and wings attached. However, the fossil insects found in amber, the fossilized gum of a tree, usually consist of the whole insect embedded in the sap. These ready-mounted specimens present ideal subjects for study. They can be easily classified.

A few years ago some lime formations were found in an old, dry lake bed. When these formations were dissolved in a weak acid, beautifully preserved insects, mites and spiders were found inside. They were not flattened, and many were not distorted, so that perfect castings of the animals remain.

One discovery showed that a fossil American snout butterfly is very close to an African species and differs only in minor details from our American species pictured on this page. The name *Dichora*, meaning "an inhabitant of two lands," has been given to the African species because it is so closely related to the fossil American butterfly.

The living snout butterflies are distinguished by the long jointed organs on either side of the front of the head that project forward to form a pronounced snout or beak. They also have squared-off tips to their fore wings. The snout butterflies are remarkable because they belong to a family which is represented in the five major geographic divisions of the world, yet there is only one genus and usually but a single species in any one locality. This is true of North America.

Our snout butterfly is one of the species that sometimes migrate in great swarms. Several such migrations have been observed in Texas, the last in 1925. The caterpillar is dark velvety-green, striped with yellow. The first two sections of the body are arched up over the head to form a hump. On the hump is a pair of black bumps with a yellow ring at the base. The caterpillars, like those of the Emperor or Hackberry butterflies, eat hackberry.

51

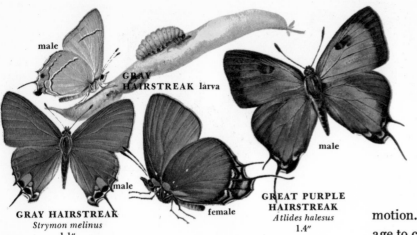

male

GRAY
HAIRSTREAK larva

male

GRAY HAIRSTREAK
Strymon melinus
1.1"

male

female

**GREAT PURPLE
HAIRSTREAK**
Atlides halesus
1.4"

male

COLORADO HAIRSTREAK
Hypaurotis chrysalus
1.5"

Hairstreaks

The hairstreaks, coppers, elfins, blues and harvesters all belong to a large, world-wide family. All are small and included among them is our smallest North American species, the Pigmy Blue. Some are rapid, strong fliers but many are dainty, weak little butterflies. Nearly all have some blue, copper or green on the wings. These colors are iridescent; they change in hue as light on them changes. Most of the flattened, slug-shaped caterpillars feed on plants. A few feed on mealy bugs and plant lice. A small number produce "honeydew," a sweet-tasting fluid, and live in close relationship with ants (p. 59). Some actually live in ant nests. Except for a few species, the hairstreaks have one or more slender tails on their hind wings. The name "hairstreak," however, comes from the fine, streaky lines on the undersides of the wings.

The Gray or Common Hairstreak is a swift-flying, rather dull-colored little butterfly. It is probably the commonest hairstreak. Both the upper and lower surfaces of the wings are blue-gray, the upperside being darker than the underside. This butterfly covers a wide territory, from the Far West across the continent, into Central America, and in the West Indies. It feeds on flowers, preferring clover, thistles, milkweed and dog-fennel. When it alights, it rubs its hind wings together in an up-and-down

motion. Sometimes the caterpillars cause damage to cultivated beans and hops and become a problem to commercial growers.

The Great Purple Hairstreak is probably our most dazzling and showy species, with brilliant iridescent colors. Like most of the hairstreaks, it prefers the tropics. Although found from Florida to New Jersey, and westward to Illinois and even California, it is nowhere common; it is very rare in the northern part of its range. The larva feeds on mistletoe, so the butterfly searches out the oaks on which this parasite grows to lay her eggs on the food plant.

The upper surfaces of the wings of the Colorado Hairstreak are a royal purple bordered in black. This species lives in southern Colorado, Utah, Arizona and southern California.

The wings of the White-M Hairstreak are iridescent blue at the base, on the upper side, with a contrasting brown underside. The hind wing is crossed by two white lines; the inner one is zigzagged and forms the letter "M" lying on its side. The caterpillar feeds on oaks and locoweed.

The California Hairstreak is present thoughout the Pacific Coast area in considerable numbers. It feeds on a great variety of flowers. Its nearest relative, the Sylvan Hairstreak, is always found around willow trees in California.

In the Gulf states a frequent visitor is the Southern Hairstreak. It sometimes gets as far north as New Jersey and West Virginia. The underside of its wings is like that of the White-M Hairstreak except for the broad, brilliant red band near the outer edge of the hind wing.

The Striped Hairstreak is easily recognized

by the widely separated broken lines on the underside of the wings. Its larva feeds on various plants, including willow, oak, juneberry, plum, apple, blackberry and blueberry.

Three species—Edward's Hairstreak, the Banded Hairstreak and the Acadian Hairstreak—look very much alike but can be told apart by the different markings on the undersides of the wings. The inner line on Edward's Hairstreak is broken up into white-edged spots placed close together; in the Acadian these spots are smaller and widely separated; in the Banded this inner line is not so broken. The Edward's Hairstreak defends its "territory" by attacking all comers.

The Red Banded or Cecrops Hairstreak is typically a butterfly of the southern states, but finds its way as far north as New York, Michigan and Indiana. The uppersides of the wings (especially of females) are blackish-brown tinted with blue at the bases. The red band across the outer third of the wings helps to further mark this butterfly.

The wide-ranging Olive Hairstreak is found from New England to Florida, west to Ontario and Nebraska and southwest to Texas. The distinctive green undersides of the wings are marked with easily seen white and brown lines. Early in the spring the butterfly lays its eggs both on the tips and on the blossoming twigs of red cedar. The eggs hatch in about a week and the larva completes its feeding in five or six weeks.

The Hedgerow Hairstreak is found in the Pacific states, mainly in the mountains. The upper surfaces of its wings are sepia; the undersides are brown with zigzag white lines.

The only common, widespread butterfly of this group that does not have tails on its hind wings is the Coral Hairstreak. It is found in open meadows and along roadsides from Georgia to Texas and north to Canada. This butterfly has a band of coral-colored spots along the outer section of the hind wing on the underside.

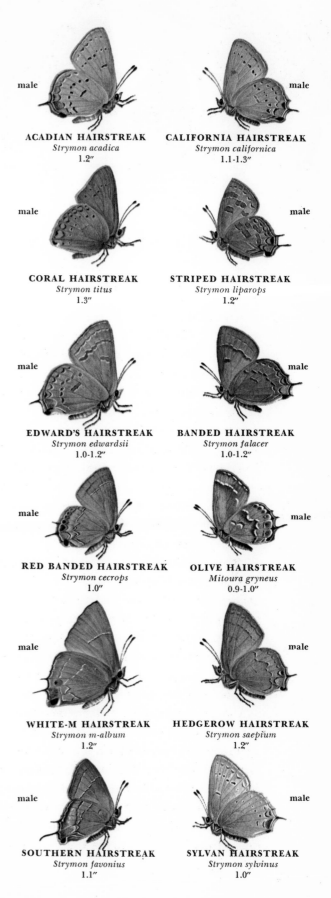

male   **ACADIAN HAIRSTREAK**   male
Strymon acadica
1.2"

male   **CALIFORNIA HAIRSTREAK**
Strymon californica
1.1-1.3"

male   **CORAL HAIRSTREAK**
Strymon titus
1.3"

male   **STRIPED HAIRSTREAK**
Strymon liparops
1.2"

male   **EDWARD'S HAIRSTREAK**
Strymon edwardsii
1.0-1.2"

male   **BANDED HAIRSTREAK**
Strymon falacer
1.0-1.2"

male   **RED BANDED HAIRSTREAK**
Strymon cecrops
1.0"

male   **OLIVE HAIRSTREAK**
Mitoura gryneus
0.9-1.0"

male   **WHITE-M HAIRSTREAK**
Strymon m-album
1.2"

male   **HEDGEROW HAIRSTREAK**
Strymon saepium
1.2"

male   **SOUTHERN HAIRSTREAK**
Strymon favonius
1.1"

male   **SYLVAN HAIRSTREAK**
Strymon sylvinus
1.0"

female

AMERICAN
COPPER larva

male

female

male

male

AMERICAN COPPER
Lycaena phlaeas americana
1.0"

GREAT COPPER
Lycaena xanthoides
1.5-1.7"

Coppers

The wings of the coppers are, as one expects from their name, a coppery color marked with darker shades. The males are usually darker and have a purplish iridescence on the uppersides of the wings. In one western species the male is bright blue, and in one form even the female has a lot of blue on the upper surfaces of its wings. Coppers are found mostly in north temperate regions, but one species lives in Central America and a few are found in Africa and the Indo-Australian region.

All too often, when writing about coppers, the experts are forced to confess: "Early stages unknown." The larvae and food plants of a few coppers are known but it is possible that the feeding relationship between the larvae of these butterflies and ants—common to some European coppers and some American blues— has not received enough attention (p. 59).

The nearest relatives of the American Copper are in Europe; as a matter of fact, the American Copper is merely a subspecies of a European butterfly. It is one of the commonest of American butterflies and is abundant except in the South and Far West. Several subspecies of this butterfly have been named and they range from the Arctic to the Gulf states. This

little butterfly will attack other butterflies as large as the Monarch as well as birds, dogs and, no doubt, anything that comes within its range! The larva, usually dull rosy-red with yellowish tints, feeds on sorrel or yellow dock. This species overwinters as a chrysalis.

The Great Copper Butterfly is one of the largest coppers in North America. The tops of the wings are a shiny brownish-gray. The underside is pale pearl-gray spotted with black and with an orange patch near the outer edge of the hind wing. This is one of the duller-colored coppers. In California, a southern mountain race of this butterfly has much lighter undersides to its wings and the black spots are much reduced in size. We know very little about the early stages of this copper. However, its food plant is known—bitter dock, a weedy plant. The Great Copper ranges from central Canada to the upper Mississippi Valley.

The wings of the male Ruddy Copper are a shiny coppery-red above. The female has the normal coloring for the group—dull, orange-yellow wings marked with brownish-black. The fringes of the wings are uniformly white, an outstanding feature of this butterfly. The underside is white and the hind wing has no black spots. This brilliant little beauty is common in the high mountains of northern California and Oregon, Nevada and Montana, where it is found on the herb plant, *Arnica*.

The uppersides of the wings of the male Purplish Copper Butterfly have tones of iridescent purple. The female's are bright yellowish-copper, spotted and edged with black. In both male and female there is a wavy orange line around the margin of the hind wing. On the underside, the fore wings are yellowish spotted with black; the hind wings are more grayish with the orange line repeated.

The Purplish Copper is one of the commonest coppers found from the Pacific Coast east to the Great Lakes. Meadowlands, roadsides and stream beds are its favorite haunts. The grass-green larva, covered with spiny bumps, feeds on dock, baby's breath and knotweed. The chrysalis is covered with delicate raised lines separated by green warty knobs that have bristles sticking out of them. The chrysalis is greenish with brown and black streaks and spots.

The Gorgon Copper, another member of this genus, lives in California and Nevada. Here it is one of the more common species, similar to some forms of the Great Copper. The wings of the male, however, have a more shiny red color above; those of the female are more broadly mottled with a pale reddish color, and the spots in some specimens are buff or tan. The Gorgon Copper prefers mountainous regions but is found occasionally in the lowlands. Nothing is known about the early stages of this copper.

The Bronze Copper is another one of our largest coppers. The uppersides of the male's wings are yellow-brown with a strong rusty shading and purplish iridescence. The uppersides of the female's wings are orange-yellow marked with brownish-black. The distinctive features of both the male and female of this copper are the broad orange-red band around the edges of the hind wings, and the silvery-gray undersides of the hind wings. The Bronze Copper has a wide range from eastern Canada south to Pennsylvania and New Jersey, then westward to midwestern Canada, Nebraska and Colorado.

The Bronze Copper prefers low, grassy meadows, especially those that are wet for at least part of the year. It may even be found along the edges of salt marshes. The species is noted for its rapid flight near the ground, but it rarely travels far from its food plant.

The pale green eggs of the Bronze Copper butterfly are laid twice a year, in early July and again in September. The inch-long, slug-shaped caterpillar is yellowish-green with a dark green stripe on its back. It feeds on sorrel. The chrysalis is yellowish-brown. There are two broods each year. Adults are found in June and in August. The winter is spent in the egg stage and it is the August females that produce these overwintering eggs.

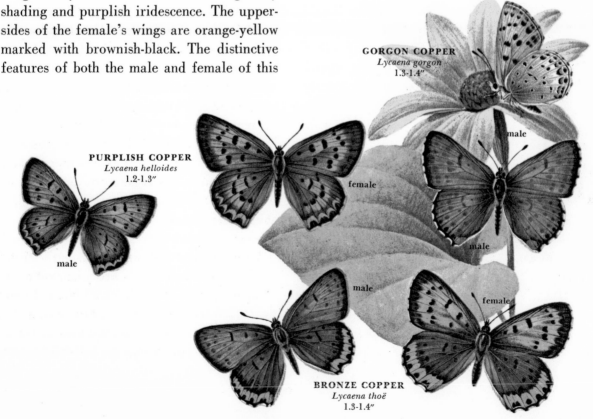

GORGON COPPER
Lycaena gorgon
1.3-1.4"

male

PURPLISH COPPER
Lycaena helloides
1.2-1.3"

female

male

male

male

male

female

BRONZE COPPER
Lycaena thoë
1.3-1.4"

Elfins

BANDED or PINE ELFIN
Incisalia niphon
0.8-1.2"
larva

male
male
larva

male

female

BANDED or PINE ELFIN

WESTERN BANDED ELFIN
Incisalia eryphon
1.2"

BROWN ELFIN
Incisalia augustinus
0.9-1.0"

male

HOARY ELFIN
Incisalia polios
0.9-1.0"

male

WESTERN ELFIN
Incisalia iroides
0.9-1.0"

male

HENRY'S ELFIN
Incisalia henrici
0.9-1.1"

male

FROSTED ELFIN
Incisalia irus
0.9-1.5"

male

These small butterflies are among the first to appear in the spring, along with the early swallowtails and Mourning Cloak. The small size of the elfins makes them difficult to see. They are rather weak fliers, although some of them are quick when frightened. The Brown Elfin, one of our common eastern species, occurs locally in large numbers, often on shrubbery.

The Brown Elfin ranges from Newfoundland to South Carolina and west to Illinois and Michigan. Its green caterpillar feeds on blueberries and sheep laurel. This elfin overwinters as a pupa.

The Banded or Pine Elfin, found from eastern Canada to Florida and west to Texas and Arkansas, has shiny dark-brown wings above and yellowish-brown underneath. Cinnamon-brown bands cross them, and some are bordered with white. Its caterpillar feeds on pine.

On the Pacific Coast, the Western Banded Elfin is slightly larger than, but similar to the Banded Elfin. Its food plant is thought to be pine. The Western Banded Elfin should not be confused with the Western Elfin, which is on the wing as early as March. The Western Elfin has a very definite lobe on the hind wings. The larva feeds on sedum.

Henry's Elfin is widely distributed but rare. This elfin has short "tails" at the edge of the hind wing. The adults show a preference for redbud and huckleberry flowers.

The Hoary Elfin can be recognized by the gray shading on the underside of its wings. It favors dry, open areas where bearberry thrives.

Rather long tails, gray "frosting" of the hind wing and a duller color below distinguish the Frosted Elfin from Henry's Elfin and from the Hoary Elfin. Lupine and false indigo are its food plants. The Frosted Elfin makes a loose cocoon in dead leaves on the ground.

Blues and Harvesters

HARVESTER
Feniseca tarquinius
1.3"

male

HARVESTER larva and pupa

aphids

EASTERN TAILED BLUE
Everes comyntas
0.9-1.1"

male

female

larva

pupa

male

WESTERN PIGMY BLUE
Brephidium exilis
0.5-0.7"

male

male

**DWARF
or EASTERN
PIGMY BLUE**
*Brephidium
isophthalma*
0.5-0.7"

male

male

male, spring

male, summer

COMMON BLUE or SPRING AZURE
Lycaenopsis argiolus
0.8-1.3"

**COMMON BLUE
or SPRING AZURE** pupa
and larva

male

female

WESTERN TAILED BLUE
Everes amyntula
0.9-1.1"

Among the oddities of the butterfly world is a little group, found the world over, in which the caterpillar feeds on other insects instead of on plants. The Harvester, also known as the Wanderer and the Alder Butterfly, is the only member living in North America. The caterpillar feeds on species of woolly aphids found on alder, beech, wild currant, hawthorn, ash, witch hazel and several other trees and shrubs. The chrysalis of the Harvester is also unusual —when seen from above, it looks very much like the head of a monkey.

The blues reach their greatest development in the Northern Hemisphere, although there are many tropical species. Most of the species are blue, but some are brown and others whitish. The Eastern Tailed Blue is one of the commonest butterflies of eastern North America. Its coloring varies according to the season, and the female is often entirely brown. The Western Tailed Blue is quite like the eastern species in many ways, but is more western in its range.

The Western and Eastern Pigmy Blues, our smallest butterflies, are quite similar. The Western Pigmy lives in our Southwest but sometimes strays as far north as Nebraska and as far south as Venezuela. The Eastern Pigmy, or Dwarf Blue, is only found in southeastern United States and the West Indies.

The Common Blue, or Spring Azure, is probably the first butterfly to emerge in the spring from its overwintering pupa. It is the most widely distributed blue on the North American continent. The adults are very pale and delicate-looking and have thin scales. The Spring Azure occurs in many striking forms. These vary both with the geographic location

ACMON BLUE
Plebeius acmon
0.7-1.0"
male
male

ORANGE BORDERED BLUE
Lycaeides melissa
0.9-1.2"
male

female

MARINE BLUE
Leptotes marinus
0.7-1.1"

male
male
male
female
male
male

REAKIRT'S BLUE
Hemiargus isolus
0.8-1.1"

and the season. The caterpillar eats a wide choice of foods and will thrive on flowering dogwood, blueberry, sumac, meadowsweet and several other shrubs.

The Acmon Blue ranges widely throughout western United States but gets only as far east as Nebraska, Kansas and Minnesota. The color of the males differs from that of the females. The males are blue above; the females brown. The males' wings have orange bands along the edges. The black-spotted, yellowish larva has a green stripe along its back. It feeds on vetch, locoweed, trefoil and other legumes. Reakirt's Blue is one of the eyed blues—it has black eye-spots on its hind wings. The uppersides of the male wings are lilac blue. The female's wings are brownish-gray with a touch of blue at their bases. The larvae feed on the spiny shrub mesquite in the Southwest and Mexico.

One of the distinctive features of the beautiful Orange Bordered Blue is that the females have a band of orange-red crescents on the edges of all wings. The males have blue wings with a narrow black line along the margin and white fringes. One of the tropical blues, the Marine Blue, is common in Mexico and ranges

north to Kansas, where it breeds but cannot overwinter. It is also found in California and is common in southern Texas, where it is on the wing from April to December.

Another handsome small butterfly is the Sonora Blue. The wings are silvery-blue above with black edges, and each wing of the female has a splash of orange-red near the outer edge; the male has orange-red spots only on the fore wings. The underside is a mottled gray and the fore wings are spotted-black. The larva of the Sonora Blue feeds on stonecrop and so is found in small colonies located only where this peculiar plant grows.

The Silvery Blue is identified by the shining silvery-blue color on the upperside of the wings. It is found over a wide area and many forms of it occur. The larvae are carefully attended by ants.

Another brightly shining species is the Saepiolus Blue, also known as the Greenish Blue because the wings of the male have flashes of brilliant green. The female's wings are darkish above with greenish-blue scales at the base. The food of the caterpillar is clover.

In the Pacific Coast states is the Square-spotted Blue, small and attractive with square-shaped, dark spots on the undersides of the wings. Nothing is known about the early stages of this little blue. So little is known of this and other small butterflies that an interested and careful observer could make a worthwhile scientific contribution by breeding and rearing them.

An association with other insects is not always harmful to butterflies. For example, the whole development of the Harvester larva takes only 10 or 11 days; this is probably because it feeds on insects, which provide more nourishment than plants. When the association of butterfly and insect involves cooperation, the relationship is useful and helpful to both.

This type of relationship reaches its highest development in the blues, such as the Silvery Blue, which have a kind of mutual aid arrange-ment with ants. Many of the larvae of the blues have a gland on the back of the seventh body segment from which they produce "honey-dew," a sweet-tasting fluid. When it is present, this gland can be seen in the last, or next to the last, larval stage, but in some species the larva produces the honeydew after the second molt. Ants stay with these larvae and protect them from other insects and parasites that might attack them. The ants touch or stroke the honey-dew gland, which then produces a drop of the sweet juice for the ants to drink. Ants always treat the caterpillars with care. They have been discovered bringing the caterpillars to food plants near ant nests; in this way the ants put the larvae to pasture for other ants to share. Some species of blues are as dependent on ants as domestic animals are on man, and cannot live without them.

SILVERY BLUE
Glaucopsyche lygdamus
0.9-1.2"

SAEPIOLUS BLUE
Plebeius saepiolus
0.9-1.2"

SONORA BLUE
Philotes sonorensis
0.9"

SQUARE-SPOTTED BLUE
Philotes battoides
1.0-1.1"

Skippers

The skippers are a large, world-wide group of butterflies that is particularly well developed in North and South America and in the Indo-Malayan region. More than 2,000 kinds have been identified, and in some districts in South America more than 50% of the butterfly species are skippers. In the United States the skippers fall into two families: the true skippers

LONG TAILED SKIPPER
Urbanus proteus
1.6-2.0"

male

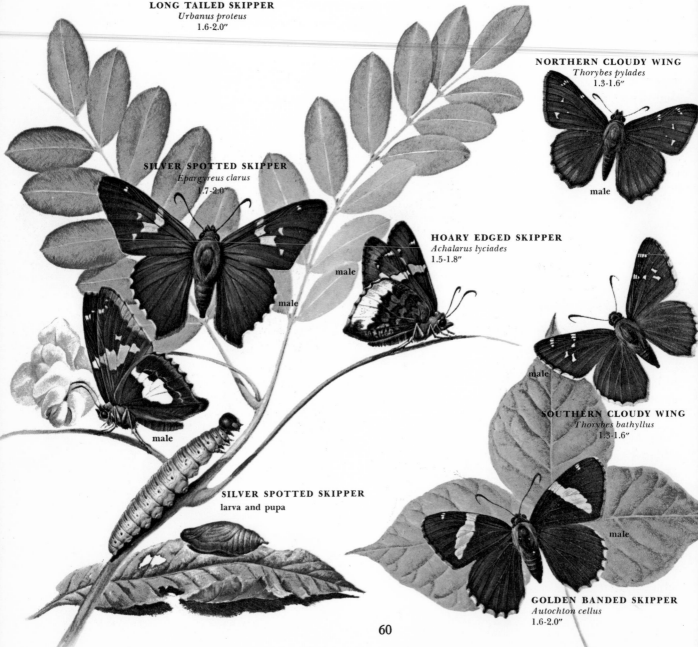

NORTHERN CLOUDY WING
Thorybes pylades
1.3-1.6"

male

SILVER SPOTTED SKIPPER
Epargyreus clarus
1.7-2.0"

male

male

HOARY EDGED SKIPPER
Achalarus lyciades
1.5-1.8"

male

male

SOUTHERN CLOUDY WING
Thorybes bathyllus
1.3-1.6"

male

SILVER SPOTTED SKIPPER
larva and pupa

GOLDEN BANDED SKIPPER
Autochton cellus
1.6-2.0"

male

and the giant skippers. The giant skippers are only found in the New World.

All of the skippers have thick bodies, with rather broad heads and antennae that usually end in a hook. The wings are short in proportion to the heavy bodies. This probably accounts for the short, strong, swift strokes of the wings and the quick, skipping, darting flight—which gives these butterflies their name—so characteristic of the group. The caterpillars of skippers are different from all others. They generally have smooth bodies and large heads shaped like a globe or pyramid. The first segment back of the head is very thin, giving the caterpillar a "neck." The pupa is usually formed between two leaves that have been drawn together with silk. It is wrapped in a loose cocoon and attached to the leaf stem by a loop. The larvae of the giant skippers do not form their pupae in this way. They are borers into yucca and related plants, and pupation occurs in a tunnel cut by the larva.

The Long Tailed Skipper is really a tropical butterfly. It is found all over the warmer parts of the Americas but occasionally strays as far north as Connecticut. The caterpillar feeds on peas, beans and similar plants and is sometimes destructive to cultivated legumes. When this happens, it is referred to as the "bean-leaf roller" or "roller worm."

The Silver Spotted Skipper is found over much of the United States, where it is a common visitor to gardens. Its flight is rapid, but the butterfly often stops at flowers. Black locust, honey locust, wistaria and related plants are the foods of the larva. Both the Hoary Edged Skipper and the Silver Spotted Skipper have golden patches on their fore wings, but the white patch of the Hoary Edged Skipper is closer to the edge. Legumes are the food for the larva. Their range is from New England to Florida, and west to Iowa down to Texas.

The clear, unbroken yellow band of the fore wing marks the Golden Banded Skipper. This butterfly is unusually sluggish for a skipper,

and spends much time at flowers. The Northern Cloudy Wing and Southern Cloudy Wing are similar species with so nearly the same range that they could easily have been given the same name. The broader white bars on the fore wing of the Southern Cloudy Wing are its best field marks.

The many dusky wings in our country are difficult to tell apart. Many are common and widespread, and may be seen from early spring through the summer. Their flight is rapid and darting but does not last long. They stop often to visit flowers. The Mournful Dusky Wing and the Funeral Dusky Wing both have white fringes on their hind wings. The Funeral is found in eastern United States and the Mournful occurs farther west in Arizona, California and Mexico. The narrow fore wing of the Funeral is distinctive.

Juvenal's Dusky Wing is another widespread species found westward to the Rockies and is noted for its variable markings. Martial's Dusky Wing is not very common but is

MARTIAL'S DUSKY WING
Erynnis martialis
1.0-1.3"

JUVENAL'S DUSKY WING
Erynnis juvenalis
1.2-1.8"

MOURNFUL DUSKY WING
Erynnis tristis
1.3-1.4"

FUNERAL DUSKY WING
Erynnis funeralis
1.3-1.3"

seen more in the South. Its markings are strong and mottled. The Sleepy and the Dreamy Dusky Wings are dark species both lacking white spots on the forewings. Both are seen early in the spring. The Sleepy is found more to the south than is the slightly smaller Dusky.

The Least Skipper is quite different, a weak-flying skipper. Its tawny-orange wings announce its presence as it flies close to the ground. The grass-green larva likes grasses,

where it is well hidden. It is found from southern Canada to Florida and Texas.

Another pair of similar skippers are the Common Sooty-Wing and the Southern Sooty-Wing. The Common Sooty-Wing has more white on the fore wing than the Southern Sooty-Wing and the edges of the wings are smooth. The edges of the wings of the Southern Sooty-Wing are wavy and the wings are mottled. While the Common Sooty-Wing likes open spaces, the Southern Sooty-Wing prefers woods. Both feed on pigweed and the larva of the Common Sooty-Wing also likes lamb's quarters and tumbleweed.

The common and widespread Checkered Skipper is apt to be seen anywhere. It seldom pauses in its fast, jerky flight to feed at flowers,

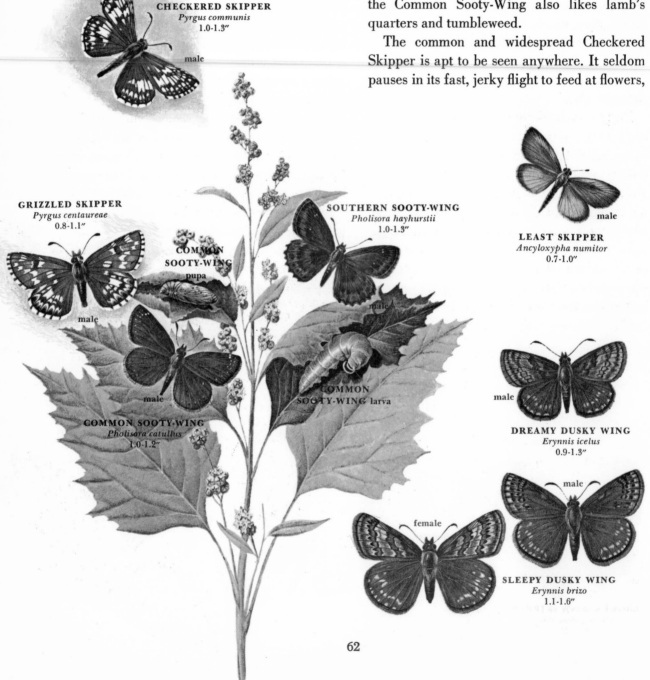

CHECKERED SKIPPER
Pyrgus communis
1.0-1.3″
male

GRIZZLED SKIPPER
Pyrgus centaureae
0.8-1.1″
male

COMMON SOOTY-WING
pupa

COMMON SOOTY-WING
Pholisora catullus
1.0-1.2″
male

SOUTHERN SOOTY-WING
Pholisora hayhurstii
1.0-1.3″
male

COMMON SOOTY-WING larva

LEAST SKIPPER
Ancyloxypha numitor
0.7-1.0″
male

DREAMY DUSKY WING
Erynnis icelus
0.9-1.3″
male

SLEEPY DUSKY WING
Erynnis brizo
1.1-1.6″
female   male

62

COBWEB SKIPPER
Hesperia metea
1.0-1.3"

male

UNCAS SKIPPER
Hesperia uncas
1.0-1.4"

male

male

INDIAN SKIPPER
Hesperia sassacus
1.0-1.4"

male

JUBA SKIPPER
Hesperia juba
1.3-1.4"

male

but is fond of sunning itself on twigs or rocks with half-open wings. It is supposed to be pugnacious, driving away butterflies that are much larger than itself. The caterpillar feeds on hollyhock and other mallows. The typical form of the Grizzled Skipper is found in Scandinavian countries, but it is found in North America also.

The Cobweb Skipper appears on the wing early in the spring. It is of a generally dark color, with white-lined veins beneath. The butterfly is found where its food plants, grasses, are plentiful. The unchanging ground color of the undersides of the hind wings, on which the white spots stand out boldly, distinguishes Juba from the Uncas Skipper. The white spots of Uncas are edged with black and there is white scaling along the veins. Both are western butterflies; the Uncas is more common on the

plains. The Indian Skipper is an eastern species that appears early in the spring.

The food plants of the skippers on this page are all the same—grasses—and we wonder how the butterflies themselves developed such a variety of forms. Though adults and caterpillars differ, they all use the same limited diet. Leonard's Skipper is noted for the underside of its hind wing, red with cream-colored spots, which it displays while feeding on the tall flowers it favors. The Golden Skipper, or Orange Skipperling, is a common Texas species. The pupa of this butterfly is odd—it has a long, slender, sharp horn on the front of its head. The Broken Dash and Long Dash Skippers are somewhat similar, but in the Long Dash the dark, central "dash" is unbroken and there is a dark area near the tip of the fore wing.

GOLDEN SKIPPER
Copaeodes aurantiaca
0.7-1.0"

male

female

LONG DASH SKIPPER
Polites mystic
1.0-1.3"

male

BROKEN DASH SKIPPER
Wallengrenia otho
0.9-1.2"

female

male

male

LEONARD'S SKIPPER
Hesperia leonardus
1.1-1.4"

63

VERNAL SKIPPER
Polites verna
0.9-1.3"

male

male

PECK'S SKIPPER
Polites peckius
0.9-1.0"

female

FIERY SKIPPER
Hylephila phyleus
1.0-1.3"

male

female

male

FIELD SKIPPER
Atalopedes campestris
1.2-1.4"

EUFALA SKIPPER
Lerodea eufala
0.9-1.1"

male

OCOLA SKIPPER
Panoquina ocola
1.0-1.4"

ROADSIDE SKIPPER
Amblyscirtes vialis
0.8-1.1"

male

male

BRAZILIAN SKIPPER
Calpodes ethlius
1.8-2.3"

male

The peculiar feature of the Vernal Skipper, or Little Glassy Wing, is that the pale spots on the fore wing have few scales and so are nearly transparent. Peck's Skipper can be recognized by its small size and by the large, light-colored patch on the underside of the hind wing. This skipper is common from eastern Canada to Texas. The Fiery Skipper is recognized by its bright, flashing, orange-yellow color above and by the yellow rays running to the edges of the wings.

The glassy, white spots of the female are characteristic of the Field Skipper. The caterpillar of this skipper feeds on grasses, as one would expect, but has a slightly different habit from the others. It makes a "tent" at the base of a leaf, then carries bits from the tip of the leaf to the tent. This species is chiefly tropical but it strays as far north as New York and the Dakotas and as far west as California.

The group to which the Eufala Skipper belongs consists of a number of similar species that can be told apart safely only by an expert. The Roadside Skipper has a violet-gray clouding on the hind wing and on the tip of the fore wing on the underside that sets it apart from other skippers in the area. When at rest, on stones, ground or flowers, the Roadside Skipper holds its wings out at an angle and turns its antennae in small circles. The southern Ocola Skipper ranges north to Ohio, Indiana and New York, but is common only in the south. The Brazilian Skipper's established home is from Florida to Texas and south to Argentina. There are records of it, however, from California, New York, Missouri and Washington, D.C. Various species of cannas provide food for the larva.

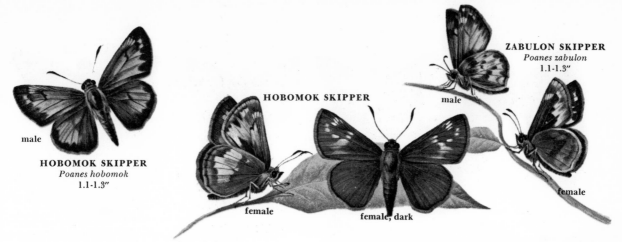

ZABULON SKIPPER
Poanes zabulon
1.1-1.3"
male

HOBOMOK SKIPPER

male

HOBOMOK SKIPPER
Poanes hobomok
1.1-1.3"

female

female, dark

female

The male Hobomok Skipper differs strikingly from the female. The male, female and dark female pictured show the variation in this species. It is this sort of variation in skippers that sometimes causes difficulty in identification. This is particularly so when there is another kind, such as the Zabulon Skipper, which is often confused with the Hobomok.

Of the more than 225 kinds of North American skippers, only a small fraction are illustrated here, but they show the great variety found in the family. Among the many skippers in North and South America are several which closely resemble skippers from Africa and India. One kind from Brazil is almost an exact match with one from West Africa; one from Mexico is almost identical with another from India. Perhaps these likenesses are due to the development of skippers in similar environments, thousands of miles apart. Or they may be the result of the supposed drifting apart of the continents of Africa and South America millions of years ago, but after these different species of skippers had developed.

Giant Skippers

Compared with the true skippers, the giant skippers are a very small family. All of them are restricted to the New World. They are large-sized, compared to true skippers, with narrow heads. The larvae are borers and so are not easily seen. In the United States the giant skippers are mainly southern butterflies. Best known of our species is the Yucca Skipper which is typical of the giant skipper family. The caterpillar bores into the leaf bases or stems of yucca or agave plants. The larvae of some species prepare exit holes at the ends of tunnels they make in the stem; other species

YUCCA SKIPPER
Megathymus yuccae
1.8-3.3"

male

prepare exit holes in the ground at a little distance from the food plants. The Yucca Skipper occurs in several forms; it is generally dark in color with white or yellow spots. It is large, and has a swift and powerful flight. Its range is in the southern part of our country from Florida westward to Texas. Other species occur in the Southwest and in Mexico.

SOME BOOKS
ON BUTTERFLIES

For more detailed information on butterflies, the following books will be useful.

THE BUTTERFLIES OF VIRGINIA
by A. H. Clark and L. F. Clark,
Smithsonian Misc. Coll., Vol. 116, No. 7, 1951.
An excellent but technical volume useful for most of eastern North America.

A BUTTERFLY IS BORN
by Jean Pierre vanden Eeckhoudt
Sterling, 1959
The life cycle of a butterfly shown in excellent photographs. (Y)

BUTTERFLIES
by E. B. Ford
Collins, 1957
This is a volume on British butterflies, rich in basic information. Many species in North America are similar.
Illustrations include color plates.

THE WORLD OF BUTTERFLIES AND MOTHS
by Alexander B. Klots
McGraw-Hill, 1958
This book, built around beautiful French color plates, gives an overall, popular vista of lepidoptera.

A FIELD GUIDE TO THE BUTTERFLIES
OF NORTH AMERICA
by Alexander B. Klots
Houghton Mifflin, 1951
This is a standard field guide to species east of the Rockies.

AMERICAN BUTTERFLIES AND MOTHS
by Cecile H. Matschat
Random House, 1942
A large, easy-to-read book, with attractive color plates, on common species

THE STORY OF A SWALLOWTAIL BUTTERFLY
by Robert M. McClung
Morrow, 1953
How a caterpillar emerges from its egg, grows, becomes a pupa and finally appears as a mature swallowtail butterfly. (Y)

WHAT BUTTERFLY IS IT?
by Anna Pistorius
Follett, 1949
Answers commonly asked questions about growth, size, life and origins of butterflies. (Y)

INSECTS IN THEIR WORLD
by Su Zan N. Swain
Garden City, 1955
How to observe, identify and collect butterflies and moths in addition to other insects. (Y)

Books marked (Y) are particularly recommended for younger readers.

INDEX

*Page numbers in **boldface** type refer to illustrations.*

68

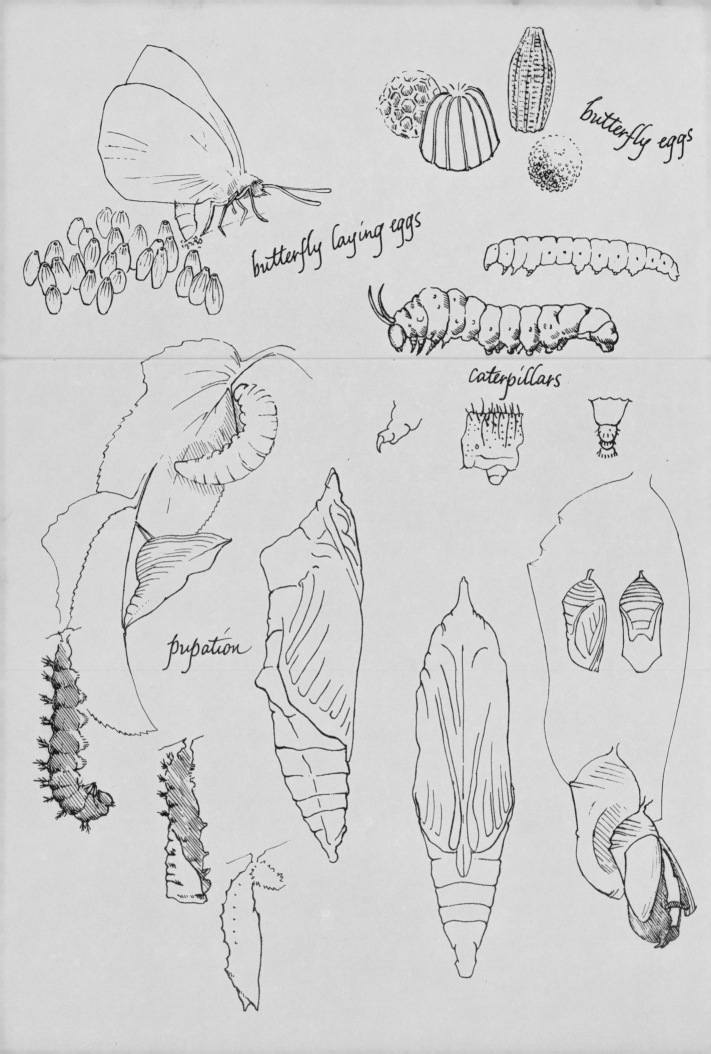

butterfly eggs

butterfly laying eggs

caterpillars

pupation